I1012979

CULPEPER

GUIDES

HOW TO GROW
HERBS

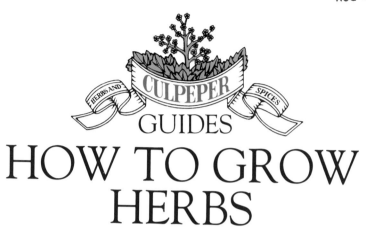

CULPEPER
HERBS AND · SPICES
GUIDES

HOW TO GROW HERBS

IAN THOMAS

General Editor
IAN THOMAS

BROCKHAMPTON PRESS
LONDON

First published in Great Britain 1988 by
Webb & Bower (Publishers) Limited

This edition published 1999 by Brockhampton Press,
a member of Hodder Headline PLC. Group

ISBN 1 86019 8058

Designed by Ron Pickless

Production by Nick Facer/Rob Kendrew

Illustrations by Antonia Enthoven

Text Copyright © 1988 Ian Thomas
Culpeper Trade Mark Copyright © 1988 Culpeper Limited
Design and layout Copyright © 1988 Webb & Bower (Publishers) Limited

Printed at Oriental Press, Dubai, U.A.E.

CONTENTS

INTRODUCTION

This book is based on the premise that you want to grow herbs and want to know the best way to grow them. Many people have been misled to believe that herbs are rather difficult to grow. This is not surprising. Herbs have been hyped, made a cult, very often by people who would find it difficult to recognise a fresh herb unless it was parsley or mint; and who have never soiled their hands growing anything. Be reassured. Most herbs are surprisingly easy to grow. The exceptions such as basil and tarragon are covered in detail in this book. If you follow the step by step instructions, you will become your own herb expert.

The herbs listed are ones that will fill your garden with interesting plants, happy flowers and aromatic leaves; scent the air of your garden and home fragrantly; encourage bees and butterflies; give you a rich variety of flavourings in your cooking; improve your family's digestion considerably; increase their resistance to ailments; and give you a simple medicine chest that will do your family a power of good and not cost you a penny. If there was however just one reason why you should grow herbs,* it is this: your health and that of your family starts in your kitchen. 'A good cook is half a physician', said Nicholas Culpeper. A good diet is essential to good health. Herbs are an essential part of a healthy diet.

The herbs are listed alphabetically together with what Culpeper would have called their 'vertues'. The growing information at the beginning is applicable to most other garden plants as well as herbs. Refer to a specific herb listing if you suspect any difficulty.

You simply cannot have enough herbs. So never worry about growing too many! Herbs in pots make lovely presents for friends. Make your own vinegars from fresh green herbs. Herb butters freeze well and you can even save fresh basil for winter use by storing the herb in oil.

Ian Thomas

'What was Paradise? But a Garden, an Orchard of trees and herbs, full of pleasure, and nothing there but delights.'
William Lawson *A New Orchard and Garden*, 1618

Growing Herbs

Growing Herbs from Pots

Many people start to grow herbs when they are attracted by a display at their local garden centre and buy a few plants already growing in a pot. This is certainly the quickest way since some perennials may be over a year old. If the plants you have bought have been grown properly, you will be off to a flying start.

Before you buy, look carefully at what you are buying. Some growers plant several small plants in a pot to give the appearance of a bushy plant. This will not develop well. In some cases, plants have been over-forced in a greenhouse so that they have become leggy and floppy. These are not a good buy either. What you should be looking for is a sturdy, well grown, bushy plant grown by a specialist grower whose livelihood depends on quality.

When you get your plants home, put them in a shady place and water well if the soil in the pots is dry. When planting your new plants, you should try (1) not to disturb the root-ball when you take each plant out of the pot prior to planting, (2) to make sure that the plant and the new soil into which you are planting it become as one. If you are good at this, your new plant will never know it has been moved!

When you come to plant, make a hole with a trowel or hand fork for each plant that is a little bigger than the pot in which it is in. Hold the pot in one hand and put your hand over the top of the pot with your fingers on either side of the plant. Turn the pot upside down and tap the pot or its sides sharply. If the pot is flexible, squeezing it will have the same effect. The pot should now come away easily without disturbing the root-ball. Holding the plant with two hands, lower the plant into the hole. The original level of the soil on the plant should be the same level as the soil into which you are planting. It can be slightly below but never above since this will cause the plant to dry out. Fill round the plant with the loose soil and press the ground gently on all sides. Water the plant and the surrounding soil. If the weather is dry, you may need to water again until the plant is established. Plants grown on from pot plants will benefit from feeding, especially those that have been grown in a peat based compost in which there are no natural nutrients. Liquid seaweed is excellent for this purpose.

Growing Herbs from Seed

This is the most economical way to grow herbs and the only way to grow annuals. All large seed companies now have a range of the more popular culinary herbs. Specialist suppliers with extensive lists of culinary, medical and ornamental herbs are listed in the Appendix.

Seeds can be sown directly into the ground or sown in seed trays or pots. Seeds sown in the ground will not need transplanting but you will have to thin the seedlings at a later stage. Seeds sown in trays and given some protection will produce earlier plants.

Do not sow too early. There is the natural temptation at the first sight of spring or during a mild winter to get started. Your seeds will not thank you if they subsequently become frozen and waterlogged. If you leave it to the proper time, you will certainly catch the early sowers.

Sowing herb seed out of doors

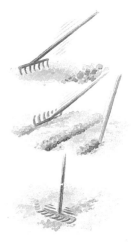

If you start in the spring wait until the ground has a little warmth and the soil is dry enough to rake. Where you sow your seeds needs to be weed-free, particularly of perennial weeds such as dock and nettle (which of course, in the right place, are excellent herbs! Not however in your seed bed). Use a fork to loosen the ground and a rake to make a fine tilth or top surface. Seeds are sown in drills or broadcast on this prepared surface. Drills are tiny, shallow trenches into which you sow the seeds covering them up with the back edge of the rake and firming the ground with the end of the rake. One way to guarantee a drill in a straight line is to put the rake flat on the ground and press down the handle. For smaller seeds, the channel created will be deep enough. For larger seeds, use the end of the rake handle to draw out a deeper channel.

Broadcast means you scatter the seeds from your hand in a sweeping motion over the ground and then rake the ground after sowing. Seeds should be watered with a can or fine spray after sowing. All weeds that compete with your seeds should be removed. Depending on how thickly you have sown your seeds, you may need to thin the seedlings as they appear to give your plants room to grow.

Growing herb seed in trays

This is much the best way, particularly as many herb seeds are very small. It gives you more control of what you sow and when you sow. Seed trays can be bought at any garden centre or you can make them from wooden orange boxes which your local store throws away. If you have no greenhouse or cold frame and want to start earlier, put your trays against the warmest wall and cover them with a framework of clear plastic film. Again, the useful orange box can be recycled for this purpose.

The seed tray should be filled with a proprietary seed compost or a mixture of your own. If using a peat based compost, you will need to watch the watering. Peat often looks damp when in fact it has dried out. Remember also that in peat based composts all the nutrients have been added. Peat on its own has no nutritional value. If your plant stays in the tray for some time (for example, while you are planting seedlings of a herb in succession), the compost may well leach off nutrients and cease to nourish your plants. Soil based composts are more natural although heavier and dirtier to handle. Soil based composts also tend to vary depending on the source of loam used in the mixture.

Why not make your own? You need first some fine soil. Moles will often provide this for you in the spring; the top of a mole hill provides beautifully worked weed free soil. Add to this grit, sharp sand and peat. Perlite, an organic inert growing medium that allows roots and cuttings to breathe, can be used instead of the grit. A good mix for herbs is five parts soil, two parts washed grit or Perlite, two parts washed sharp sand, three parts sphagnum moss peat. The aim is to have an open soil mixture that feels slightly gritty in your hands.

Fill the seed tray to a depth of 3.5cm (1½in). Bigger seeds will need greater depth since they will have longer roots. Make sure the soil is evenly spread in the tray. The corners of your tray may need levelling. If you do not do this, your valuable herb seed will vanish downhill into the corners when you water. Firm the compost gently. If using seed trays, you can use the bottom of one tray to firm the top of a filled tray. Water the tray thoroughly and leave it to stand until the surplus water has drained away.

Depending on the size of the seed being sown, you can sow individually, in little V-shaped drills or broadcast, ie sprinkling. seeds over the surface. If sowing individually or broadcast, press the seeds into the surface of the damp compost when you have finished sowing. Larger seeds are then covered using some of the compost in a fine sieve. If you have no sieve, a kitchen colander or rubbing the compost through one's hands are alternatives. The idea of covering the seed is mainly to keep it in position so a *fine* sprinkling, *just enough to make the seeds disappear* from sight is enough. If sowing in V-shaped drills, after sowing sprinkle enough fine compost to just fill the drill. Lastly, spray the top of the full seed tray with water. Your seed tray should then be covered with plastic sheeting or glass to help it retain its moisture. You may need to turn the glass from time to time to wipe away excess moisture. Seed trays should be shaded from full sun. Sheets of newspaper are ideal. Inspect your seed trays daily. Remove any covering the moment the seedlings start to emerge. It is easier to see these by looking *across* your seed tray rather than down on to it. If you do not remove the plastic cover or glass, your seedlings will become drawn and leggy. You want them short and sturdy.

Your seedlings will produce one set of leaves which started life in the seed itself. These seed leaves are quite different from the herb's normal leaves so do not worry that you may have sown the wrong seed. When the seedlings have produced a second or third set of leaves, the seedling has now grown a decent set of roots so that it can be transplanted. Transplanting is to small plant pots until the seedlings are large enough to plant in their final position in the garden. You can plant directly from the seed tray to the garden, but only if you have sown thinly enough so that your plants are not overcrowded; and let the seedlings grow stronger and bigger so that they have a good root structure that will cope with the change. If you have been growing your seedlings under protection, you will need to wean them off this for about a week before planting out. This will also apply to the seedlings you planted into small pots before these too go in the ground. To wean or 'harden off', you introduce the seedlings or plants gradually to the temperature and conditions outside. At one time, seedlings were placed in cold frames of which the covers were opened more each day. You can begin by putting your seedlings outside each day in a sheltered position; and then leaving them out at night.

To transplant seedlings, first fill the pots into which the seedlings are going. Push something thin and flat (a cake knife is ideal) under the compost and lift a block of seedlings. Separate the seedlings gently by easing them from the compost with as many roots as possible. *Never* hold seedlings round their stem. Hold them gently by their leaves. Make a hole in the compost in the pot. A dibber is ideal but anything the size and shape of your index finger will create the same hole. Drop the seedling into the hole so that the seed leaves (the first ones) are at the same level as the compost. With your dibber, or finger, or ballpoint pen, crumble the compost around the seedling and firm gently. Remember that roots grow downwards so make sure you have made a deep enough hole to take the root system of the seedling. When you have planted all your seedlings, water the pots or ground thoroughly. Use a watering can with a fine rose. *Even, thorough watering* of pots is most important at this stage otherwise your pots will dry out unevenly. How often you water from now on depends very much on the amount of sunlight. You should certainly not let your pots dry out completely. Equally, you should not overwater. How do you judge? The simplest way is to inspect the compost inside the pot by turning out the root-ball as described previously. If the bottom half is damp, water another day. You are trying to encourage the roots to grow downwards, which roots will do when they are forced to look for water. Alternatively, once the plants are better established, you can just look at the bottom of the pot itself. If it is damp, there is enough water available.

Feeding of the seedlings, whether in the ground or in pots, can start when you see signs of renewed growth.

Growing herb seeds in compartmentalised trays

These are a useful herb-growing help. Herbs grown in the individual compartments can be planted without any root disturbance. The trays are ideal for taking cuttings.

Trays available vary in size but typically a tray 52cm × 32.5cm (20in × 13in) may have 273 compartments each 20mm square (¾in square). A tray the same size may have bigger compartments but less of them: 150 each 30mm square (1in square).

Each individual compartment has a hole in the bottom. If you put your empty tray on a flat surface and pour compost over it as you would a seed tray, and then lift the tray in the air or water it, you will see that some of the compost drains out of the holes. Some holes will be empty, others uneven. What do you do to prevent this? The holes taper towards the bottom so if you firm the compost evenly in each hole before sowing or watering, the compost will not fall out. You could do this using a finger to push the soil down in each hole but this gets rather boring and you may over-compress the soil. The recommended method is to use a stiff hand brush with nylon bristles about 5cm (2in) long. Place the tray on a *firm* flat surface. Cover the tray completely with compost. Brush off the surplus compost. Lift the tray with two hands, keep the bottom of the tray level with the firm surface and bang the tray *hard* on the firm surface once or twice. This helps settle the compost in each hole. Cover the tray again. Brush off the surplus again and with the brush bristles still pointing downwards, hit the individual compartments with the bristles of the brush. Do this several times, working across the tray from left to right, top to bottom. It may take a bit of practice but you will end up with a tray in which each hole is filled with the same level of compost; and that level should be .6cm (¼in) below the top of each hole. This gives you enough room to sow your seeds and cover them when sown. Once filled, water the tray and leave it until the surplus water has drained away.

Sow the seeds into the individual holes. With slow germinating seed like parsley or chervil, sow at least two seeds per hole. If nimble-fingered, you can pick up each seed in your fingers. Alternatively, take a sheet of stiff paper, fold it and place some seeds in the fold. Hold the fold of seeds in one hand slightly downwards and tap the folded paper at the end which points down until a seed drops off into the hole. When all the holes are sown, cover the tray with fine compost, and water lightly. water lightly.

Seeds grown in compartmentalised trays will want to send their roots down through the hole at the bottom so it is a good idea to stand these trays on damp sand or gravel. When it is time to transplant the seedlings, you will need to loosen them from their individual holes. Commercial growers use the horticultural equivalent of a bed of fakir's spikes where the spikes exactly match the number and position of the holes. You can use the narrow end of your dibber or the top of a ball-point pen to push up the plants. You do not need to push out completely. Just push up slightly and you can pull the plants out one by one as you transplant. Growing in trays of this kind is much better if you want to transplant direct to the garden since there is no disturbance of the roots which are in a firm little plug.

GROWING HERBS FROM CUTTINGS

Cuttings are hard or soft wood shoots of a plant which, if put in the ground or a growing medium at the right time, will develop roots and become plants in their own right. Cuttings of herbs are usually taken from active plants, ie when the plant is growing, not dormant. Taking cuttings is the usual form of propagation for perennial herbs such as lavender, rosemary and santolina where the propagation of a distinct variety is important. If you are creating a formal garden in which lavender forms a focal part, you do not want bushes of different shapes and flowers of differing hues. This can happen when perennials are grown from seed.

Cuttings can be taken virtually at any time, providing you have some bottom heat, ie your soil or compost into which you will insert the cuttings has some heat. Before electricity this was provided by beds of manure working under a layer of soil. Today, soil warming cables are the answer. Cuttings root more easily when they are taken from strong-growing, healthy, well-fertilised plants.

Cuttings are ideally non-flowering sturdy shoots about 7.5cm (3in) long cut from the mother plant with a *sharp* knife. Cutting with a sharp knife leaves a clean edge. The cut is made just below a set of leaves. The bottom half of the cutting is stripped of *all* its leaves. The cutting thus has its top half covered in leaves, the bottom half stripped of leaves, and a clean cut just below the node where the bottom leaves were.

Commercial growers will do their cuttings in batches since allowing the cut area of the cutting to dry before putting it in the growing medium is regarded as beneficial. This is certainly true of scented geraniums which can even be left overnight without harm. You can at this stage coat the bottom of the cutting with a hormone powder to promote rooting. This is not necessary. Moreover, there is as yet no convincing evidence these chemicals work in all cases. Culpeper produce thousands of herb plants without using hormones.

The cutting is next inserted into the growing medium. Perlite is one of the best growing mediums for cuttings, either on its own or mixed 50/50 with peat. Using Perlite requires some personal care. You should not breathe in the dust. Pouring water into the bag before you use it prevents the dust. You can grow cuttings in any containers where the drainage is good. Professional growers use compartmentalised trays. The open hole allows the roots to develop and enables the grower to push out the plug containing the rooted cutting without damage to the roots. These trays can also be found at garden centres. Alternatively, fill a large pot or deep seed tray.

To put your cutting into the tray or pot, make a thin narrow hole in the growing medium with your dibber (a kitchen skewer can be used). Insert the stripped bottom half of the cutting into the hole. Firm the growing medium round the cutting with the dibber or skewer. This is best done by pushing the thin end of the dibber from the edge of the compartment towards the bottom of the cutting thus firming the compost around the cutting. When all your cuttings are planted, water well. Place in a *cool* place for twenty-four hours before introducing the cuttings to any warmth. This is to allow the cuttings which may droop initially to recover.

Besides bottom heat, cuttings need a moist atmosphere to prevent their dehydration, and shading from the strong rays of the sun until they root. Stand all your cuttings in their tray close together on a bed of damp sand or gravel under which your soil warming cable is buried. Cover the cuttings with a sheet of plastic about 45cm (18in) above the top of the cuttings. Either make a frame on which to stretch the plastic, or stretch wire on short posts and put the plastic on top of the wire. The plastic should drop down to the ground on all four sides to make a little plastic 'house' over the cuttings. Cover the plastic with sheets of paper to shield the cuttings from direct sun. Remove the paper when the sun has passed.

Water the cuttings with a watering can with a fine rose daily in hot weather, and whenever they show signs of flagging. The cutting medium does not want to be soaked but it does want to be damp. Rooting of herbs varies. Mints root within days; rosemary may take ten days; lavenders and other woody species take longer. Do not be faint hearted. As long as your cutting is upright, it is likely to root in time even if you have not invested in a soil-warming cable.

Because you are growing your cuttings in a growing medium that has no nutrients, 'when good roots show, it's time to go!'[1]. Ideally, when those good roots show, you should transplant your cuttings at once into 9cm (3.5in) pots using a good compost. If you leave the cuttings in the tray for planting later, feed them regularly to keep the cuttings in good condition.

You will have noticed the regular use of the word 'gentle'. There is no other word that aptly describes how you should handle seeds, seedlings and cuttings, particularly of tiny plants like thymes. Remember to:

[1]Mary Peddie
Second National Herb Growing and Marketing Conference, Indianapolis, July 1987.

HANDLE BY THE LEAVES NOT THE STEMS. NEVER SQUEEZE THE STEMS OF EITHER A SEEDLING OR CUTTING.

WATER THOROUGHLY SEED TRAYS, TRANSPLANTED PLANTS OR CUTTINGS THE MOMENT YOU HAVE PLANTED THEM.

PROTECT TRANSPLANTED PLANTS AND CUTTINGS FROM HOT DIRECT SUNLIGHT UNTIL ESTABLISHED.

TRANSPLANT WHEN GOOD ROOTS SHOW.

GROWING HERB PLANTS IN CONTAINERS

Herbs do well in containers: tubs, barrels, troughs, window-boxes. Drainage is all-important. Line your containers with a layer of broken bricks or rubble. A layer of well-rotted manure on top of the rubble will give your plants nourishment and provide moisture where they need it: at the roots. Fill the container with compost and plant.

Window-boxes are more suitable for the lower growing herbs: basil, chives, thyme, parsley. Remember to secure any window boxes to prevent them being blown off. Rosemary, marjoram, mints and sage need more space. Mint needs a container all of its own.

Containers will need watering daily in the summer and feeding at least once a week. It is a good idea to replant your containers with fresh soil and plants every year – although rosemary grows well in containers and can be safely left for several seasons if fed regularly in the growing period.

HOW TO DEAL WITH BUGS AND HERB DISEASES

It is true of plants, as of humans or animals, that putting them too close together will breed disease. Do not overcrowd your plantings. Allow air and light to get to your plants. Nearly all herbs like well-drained soil.

If greenfly or other aphids become a problem, you can use natural insecticides based on Pyrethrum or derris, both of which are organic and safe to use. If a plant looks really sick, pull it out and burn it before it contaminates other plants.

FEEDING HERB PLANTS

If your herb plants are growing in a good garden soil, feeding is not essential. Annuals, especially basil, are very responsive to feeding. Perennial herbs will benefit from a sprinkling of an organic fertiliser or bone meal in the spring just before the plants start growing again.

Herbs grown in containers and pots do need feeding especially if you have planted them in a peat-based compost. At Culpeper we use a seaweed supplement which makes the leaves beautifully green, and a natural cow manure liquid product which is sprayed on when watering. Liquid feeding is easy to apply since it can be mixed in a watering can. If you have access to horse or cow manure, you can make your own liquid manure by suspending a sack of manure in a tub of water. The resulting dark liquid should be diluted to the colour of straw in your watering can. Weekly feeding of herbs in containers is recommended. Daily watering may be necessary in hot weather.

HARVESTING AND STORING HERBS

You can dry, freeze and preserve herbs in vinegar and oil.

Drying is best done when the leaves or flowers are young and fresh. Leaves are usually best, ie most aromatic, just *before* the herb flowers. Flowers are best picked when fully open and early in the morning (before the bugs get up). Roots are lifted in the autumn. Roots should be washed, dried and all tops or plant material removed. Leaves and flowers should always be picked on a dry day and never immediately after rain. Never pack the herbs down into containers as you pick; nor leave herbs and flowers in heaps otherwise they will start to heat and spoil. Herb leaves and flowers can easily bruise and spoil. Handle carefully at all times. Lay the herbs out *thinly* on a drying rack somewhere warm, dark and with free circulation of air. A drying rack is a frame or tray covered in wire-netting or sacking. The herbs should not be able to fall through the material covering the frame. Plastic is not a suitable covering since the air must be able to circulate through the material. Trays can be stacked one on top of another providing there is at least 30mm (1in) or more between each tray. New trays of fresh herbs are always put *above* trays of partly dried herbs since the moisture from the herbs rises up. The herbs will need turning or shaking once every twenty-four hours to ensure they are dried evenly. Herbs are dry when they feel crisp and resilient. Roots will snap when dry. Roots will take longer to dry than herbs and may be dried in a low oven. One of the best places to dry a small amount of herbs well is the airing cupboard where the light is excluded and the temperature is constant. Herbs will usually dry here in three to four days.

Freezing does not need material that is completely dry. Since you are not going to use masses of herbs all at once, it is best to freeze tiny bags of enough herb to last one to two days. Some herbs freeze particularly well, eg parsley and the wonderful French tarragon. Wash to remove any soil (especially parsley), shake, put in the bag, express the air, seal and put in your freezer. Do put a label on each bag. Herbs look very similar when frozen.

Preserving herbs in vinegar and oil is simple to do. Wine or cider vinegar is best. Fill a glass jar with the herb or herbs of your choice. Fill with vinegar. Stand in the sun for about a week (or again put in your airing cupboard) to transfer the aroma of the herb to the vinegar. Strain the vinegar from the herbs. The more times you do this, the more flavoured will be the vinegar. Strain, bottle and label the flavoured vinegar. A final sprig of herb in each bottle looks attractive. Preserving herbs in oil (preferably olive) requires even less work. Fill a jar with your favourite herb, cover with oil, stir to get any air out and seal. If you leave the filled jar in the kitchen, the oil will soon become aromatic. When you start to use the herb, keep the jar in the refrigerator. Always make sure the herb is below the level of the oil. When the herb is finished, you will still have a wonderfully flavoured oil for your dressings.

HERBS TO GROW

Herbs are hardy or half-hardy, annuals, biennials and perennials.

Hardy herbs will generally survive most winters. Half-hardy herbs are those that should not be put out-of-doors until all danger of frost is past. Half-hardy plants will not survive out of doors without protection. If growing in the ground, they may need a protective covering of straw or leaves; or to be transplanted into pots and put under glass.

Annual herbs germinate, grow, flower and die all in one year. Biennial herbs take two years to go through the same process. Perennial herbs are those which come up every year although they may die back during the winter.

The abbreviations under **Type** in the following list are:

HA	Hardy annual
HHA	Half-hardy annual
HB	Hardy biennial
HHB	Half-hardy biennial
HP	Hardy perennial
HHP	Half-hardy perennial

ALECOST *see Costmary*

ALESPICE *see Costmary*

ANGELICA

'It is interesting to think of this angelic plant, and the holy fathers who cull it (the Carthusian monks who make the liqueur Chartreuse), being so kindly to the human race, and ever intent on defeating the wind and coaxing perspiration.'

Kettner's Book of Table, ES Dallas, 1877

Botanical name: *Angelica archangelica*   **Family:** *Apiaceae (Umbelliferae)*
Type: HB or short lived HP.   **Height:** 120–180cm (4–6in)
Position preferred: sunny position with partial shade. Likes a soil rich in humus. Plant at least 90cm (3in) apart.
When and how to sow: ideally, immediately the seeds are ripe in the late summer when germination is good. Seedlings grown at this time are large enough to over-winter whether in the ground 30cm (12in) apart or in pots for spring planting. Otherwise, sow in March-April. Germination takes two

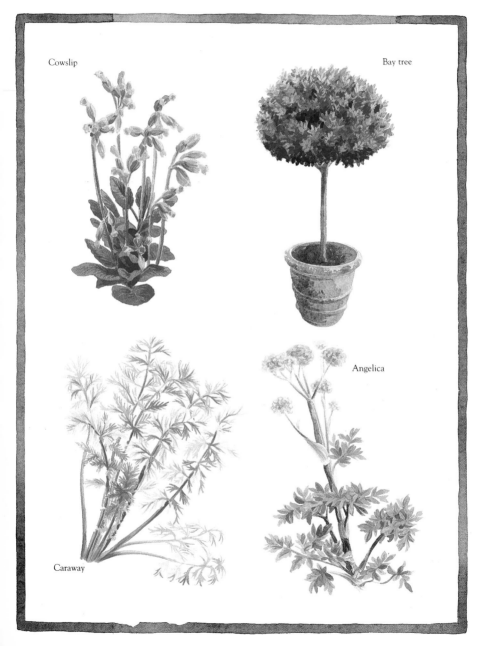

Cowslip

Bay tree

Angelica

Caraway

Bush basil, purple basil and sweet basil (green ruffles)

to three weeks and is erratic. Angelica seem to germinate better when seeds are sown together in a tray rather than individually in compartments.

When and how to propagate: seedlings around the original plant can be lifted in March or the autumn.

Leaf and flower colour and time of flowering: leaves are large and bright green. Cream heads of greenish-white flowers are produced in July–August.

Main usefulness: young stems are candied for use as cake and desserts. Add the stems to rhubarb jam. Chopped fresh leaves added to stewed fruit reduce tartness. Commercially, an essential oil produced from the seeds and roots is used to flavour shampoos, perfumes and soaps.

Other virtues: both leaf and root are used in herbal medicine. Angelica leaf tisane helps relieve flatulent dyspepsia. An infusion of the root with coltsfoot is helpful for bronchial catarrh.

How to keep for later use: candy young stems from two year plants in the spring. Dry leaves before plant flowers. Lift roots for drying in the autumn of first year.

ANISE

Botanical name: *Pimpinella anisum*   **Family:** *Apiaceae (Umbelliferae)*
Type: HA   **Height:** 30cm (1in)
Position preferred: warm, sunny position in a light dry soil.

When and how to sow: sow seed in April. Can be transplanted from trays to pots if done just after second leaves form. Otherwise, sow directly in the ground in drills 22.5cm (9in) apart. Thin to 10cm (4in).

When and how to propagate: by seeds only.

Leaf and flower colour and time of flowering: leaves are slight and feathery. White flowers form in July. Seed ripens about a month after flowering. Summer temperature needs to be above average to ripen seed.

Main usefulness: seeds are used to flavour curries, cakes and liqueurs. Leaves can be chopped and added to salads.

Other virtues: an infusion of anise seed may be used in cases of bronchial catarrh and flatulent colic. Anise seed is a useful home remedy since children like the taste.

How to keep for later use: cut whole plant at ground level when first seeds are ripe. Lay plant on paper inside airing cupboard until all seeds are ripe. Store ripe seed in sealed jar.

ARTEMISIA

see Southernwood, Tarragon, Wormwood

BASIL

'Once you have become a basil addict, it is hard to do without it.'
Elizabeth David, *Summer Cooking*, 1965

Botanical name: *Ocimum basilicum*   **Family:** *Lamiaceae (Labiatae)*
Other common name: Sweet basil
Type: HHA   **Height:** 23cm (9in)
Position preferred: full sun in well-drained soil.
When and how to sow: unless you have some heat, May is early enough. The problem is not getting the seeds to germinate. Germination is within seven days at 70°F and seeds will germinate at temperatures down to 50°F. The trouble arises when you transplant your seedlings into pots to grow them on. If the temperature should drop below about 42°F, your seedlings will almost certainly die. It is better to wait until you are sure of warmer weather. To ensure a good supply of basil, sow in succession throughout the summer either direct into the ground in drills 3–6mm (⅛–¼in) deep or in trays for transplanting. Keep the soil and seed trays moist to ensure germination. Outdoors, you will see the seeds emerge between eight and fourteen days.

Sow and thin or transplant in rows 60–90cm (24–36in) apart with plants spaced at intervals of 15cm (6in). Basil seedlings should be about 15cm (6in) tall before they are transplanted and their tops should be removed before transplanting to encourage the plant to make more branches. Basil loves its food. Feed and water well for good leaf growth. Cut off flower heads as they appear. This stops the plants setting seed and encourages continual leaf production. Basil can be grown successfully in pots and window boxes.

When and how to propagate: since basil is a herbaceous plant, cuttings can in fact be taken readily from mature plants.
Leaf and flower colour and time of flowering: aromatic, dark green shiny leaves. White flowers in small spikes in summer. Very attractive to bees.
Main usefulness: an essential ingredient for Italian cooking and all tomato dishes and salads. The main ingredient in 'pesto', a rich sauce of fresh basil, pine nuts, parmesan cheese blended in olive oil used to flavour pasta dishes. Basil is also used to flavour sausages.
Other virtues: basil is thought to be good for the stomach and a stimulant.
How to keep for later use: basil will not freeze. If you attempt to keep fresh leaves much below 45°F in your refrigerator, they will blacken. Dried basil has some flavour. Dry the whole leaves in an airing cupboard. When dry, rub the leaves between the hands and store the dried herb in

Borage and bergamot at the foot of a wall

a dark, airtight jar. Basil can be cut throughout the growing season several times. Cut at least 10–15cm (4–6in) above the ground to ensure the plant produces fresh leaves.

The best way is to preserve whole sprigs and leaves of basil in olive oil adding a little sea salt to bring out the flavour. No cooking is required and you have lovely fresh basil all winter. Save basil also in vinegar which is cheaper than using oil and just as effective if your eventual use is in a salad dressing.

Basil planted in pots in the late summer and put on a sunny window-sill will continue to produce leaves up to Christmas, sometimes beyond, providing you remove the flower heads immediately they form.

Chamomile and chervil

Other varieties: there are reputed to be over fifty types of basil. You may think you see several of these if you grow basil from seed. Seed merchants tend to mix seeds from different sources.

BUSH BASIL (*Ocimum minimum*) is a bushier, more shrub-like basil with smaller leaves. Reputed to be hardier than Sweet Basil.

FINE LEAVED or GREEK BASIL (*Ocimum minimum*) is an erect-growing, smaller-leaved form of bush basil. This is an ideal variety for tubs and window boxes. Flowers later so makes lots of leaves. Whole tender sprigs can be used in flavouring. Ideal for making basil vinegars. An American variety 'Green Bouquet' is excellent and comes true from seed. Pot some plants in the autumn for bringing into the house.

HOLY BASIL (*Ocimum sanctum*), a native of India where it is a sacred plant of the Hindu religion. Has a strong clove fragrance.

LEMON BASIL (*Ocimum citriodorum*) has bright green leaves and a strong lemon scent.

LETTUCE LEAVED BASIL (*Ocimum basilicum* var. *lactucafolium*) originated in Italy where it is also called 'monstrous leaved'. It has crinkled leaves up to 7.5cm (3in) across.

PURPLE BASIL (*Ocimum basilicum* var. *aurauascens*) is traditionally listed as a flower in seed catalogues since it is grown for use as an ornamental bedding plant. It has pale purple flowers and deep purple foliage. 'Dark Opal' and 'Purple Ruffles' are named varieties. Unless the flowerheads are removed, purple basil is finished by mid-September. Use in the kitchen as other basils.

BAY

'This is indeed poetry in the pot – Daphne at our lips.'

ES Dallas, *Kettner's Book of Table*, 1877

Botanical name: *Laurus nobilis*   **Family:** *Lauraceae*
Type: Hardy (when established) evergreen tree
Height: 4m (13ft)
Position preferred: sheltered position away from cold east and north winds. Good soil and full sun.
When and how to sow: viable seed is virtually impossible to obtain. If you can obtain it, the seeds will need stratification, ie the outer skin needs rubbing to weaken it, so assisting germination. Germination is assisted by bottom heat. Seeds are large and best planted together about 3cm (1in) each way, 2.5cm (1in) deep in a seed tray. Sow in the spring.
When and how to propagate: stem cuttings can be taken May–September. Cuttings taken from the bottom half of the bay do better

than those taken from the top. Woody stem cuttings have a better rooting chance than softer tip material. Bay cuttings need to be grown with bottom heat and kept covered in a close atmosphere. Root formation is slow so be patient.

Leaf and flower colour and time of flowering: the new season's bright green leaves turn dark green as the season progresses. Leaves are aromatic fresh or dried. White 'burned' edging to the leaves is the sign of wind and frost damage. Small yellow flowers in May. Seed may ripen in a hot summer.

Main usefulness: an essential ingredient of 'bouquet garni'. Fresh or dried leaves are crushed and added to soups (especially lentil, pea and ham), stews and rice puddings.

Other virtues: bay helps expel wind. It is good for the stomach. Its astringency helps to rid the body of fat.

How to keep for later use: dry new young leaves or use fresh throughout the winter. Bay leaves are ideally grown in tubs. These should be brought inside during frosty spells since young trees are particularly susceptible to frost damage. Frost scorches leaves or whole branches and spoils the shape of a trained tree. It is not necessary to water trees kept under cover until the spring.

BERGAMOT

Botanical name: *Monarda didyma*   **Family:** *Lamiacaea (Labiatae)*
Other common names: Bee balm, Oswego tea, Scarlet Monarda.
Type: HP   **Height:** 1m (over 3ft)
Position preferred: sunny position with some slight shade. Bergamots like a cool root run. Compost or manure should be worked into the soil before planting.
When and how to sow: sow in March–April in a seed tray 6mm (¼in) deep and transplant the seedlings when the true leaves are well formed.
When and how to propagate: split the roots of established plants in the spring and autumn. Plant 37.5cm (15in) apart.
Leaf and flower colour and time of flowering: hairy mid-green leaves that unfortunately get covered in mildew in the autumn. Spectacular bright scarlet honeysuckle-shaped flowers produced as a cluster on the end of upright stems from June to September. The whole plant has a lemon-orange scent, similar to bergamot oil which is not produced from the herb but from the fruit of *Citrus aurantium*. Bergamot is very attractive to bees.
Main usefulness: young leaves can be used fresh or dried as a refreshing tea; or to flavour jellies, wine and fruit cups, fruit salads. Use dried leaves and flowers in pot-pourri.

Coltsfoot, chive, garlic chive and chicory

Other virtues: bergamot contains thymol, a powerful antiseptic. Bergamot is used as a medicine against colds.

How to keep for later use: dry young leaves early in the season.

Other varieties:

LEMON BERGAMOT (*Monarda citriodora*) has lemon-scented leaves, purple or yellow flowers. Grows to 80cm (32in).

WILD BERGAMOT (*Monarda fistulosa*) has grey-mauve flowers.

BORAGE

'A great Cordial, great strengthener of Nature.'

Nicholas Culpeper, 1652

Botanical name: *Borago officinalis* **Family:** *Boraginaceae*

Type: HA **Height:** up to 1m (over 3ft)

Position preferred: sunny position, all soils.

When and how to sow: under glass, in trays March onwards. Outdoors, plant from April onwards. Seeds are quite big and are sown 6mm (¼in) deep. Plants should be about 45cm (18in) apart.

When and how to propagate: by seed only. Plants will often self-seed after flowering. Sow at intervals throughout the summer.

Leaf and flower colour and time of flowering: downy pale green leaves on prickly stems. Intense blue star-shaped flower with a black centre as early as May onwards. Seeds ripen overnight.

Main usefulness: leaves add a cool cucumber flavour to summer punches. Flowers can be used for decoration in salads and drinks. Flowers can be candied. Stems can be peeled and used in salads.

Other virtues: borage was regarded by herbalists as a herb that would cheer the spirits and body. Recent research shows that borage seed is a rich source of gamma linolenic acid (GLA) reported to be helpful in cases of pre-menstrual stress, eczema and other skin diseases.

How to keep for later use: dry the leaves, crumble and store.

CARAWAY

'A most admirable remedy for such as are troubled with wind.'

Nicholas Culpeper, 1652

Botanical name: *Carum carvi* **Family:** *Apiacae (Umbelliferae)*

Type: HB **Height:** 1m (over 3ft)

Position preferred: well-drained fertile soil in full sun. Caraway dies back its first winter.

When and how to sow: sow in late summer/early autumn to flower the following May. Sow broadcast or in shallow drills 30cm (1ft) apart where plants are to flower. Thin to give 15cm (6in) between each plant. Can be transplanted but only when seedlings are small. Seeds sown in the spring will flower the following May.

When and how to propagate: by seed only.

Flower colour and time of flowering: creamy-white flowers in May.

Main usefulness: seeds are used to flavour cakes. Leaves can be added to salads, soups and stews. Root is also edible and cooked like parsnips.

Other virtues: an infusion of powdered seeds is a useful home remedy for indigestion, colic and diarrhoea. Use as a gargle for laryngitis.

How to keep for later use: seeds are usually ripe by the end of July. Harvest when seed colour changes to brown. Cut plant below seed heads, spread on paper and dry in warm place. Store ripe seed in airtight containers.

CATMINT

'Cats are very much delighted herewith; for the smell of it is so pleasant to them, that they rub themselves upon it, and waller and tumble in it, and also feed on the branches and leaves very greedily.'

John Gerarde, *The Herball*, 1633

Botanical name: *Nepeta cataria*   **Family:** *Lamiaceae (Labiatae)*

Other common names: catnip and catnep

Type: HP   **Height:** 1m (3ft 4in)

Position preferred: well-drained soils in sun.

When and how to sow: sow March to May in a seed tray 6mm (¼in) deep. Transplant to small pots. Plant in final position 38cm (15in) apart.

When and how to propagate: cuttings of young shoots in the spring.

Leaf and flower colour and time of flowering: soft, downy, grey-green leaves. Spikes of white hooded flowers spotted with purple. Very attractive to bees.

Main usefulness: catmint tea is used to treat colic in children; and for colds, headache and insomnia.

Other virtues: all parts of the herb are extremely attractive to cats apparently sending them on hallucinatory 'trips'. (Some claim it does the same to humans if smoked.) As reported in *The Herbalist*, the always interesting annual publication of The Herb Society of America, considerable research has been done into what is called the 'catnip response'. The article cites eighty-two references. Cats will play with a fabric 'mouse' stuffed with the dried herb in four stages and the article reports this sequence is almost invariable: (1) sniffing, (2) licking and chewing with head shaking, (3) cheek and chin rubbing, (4) head-over rolling and body rubbing. Cats normally eat the herb when finally destroying the 'mouse'.

How to keep for later use: dry young leaves for making tea. Cut flowering stems for dried flower arrangements. Cut and dry all parts when harvesting for cats.
Other variety:

LEMON CATMINT (*Nepeta cataria* var. *citriodorum*) has an added lemon fragrance. The leaves are a softer green and the plant is less hardy.
Note: *Nepeta mussini* is of the same family and commonly found in gardens as an edging plant. Grows up to 30cm (1ft) with spikes of mauve-blue flowers from June to September. It is a more attractive garden plant than *Nepeta cataria*. There are several named varieties.

CHAMOMILE

'It is so much drunk by American women after lunch instead of coffee that it is now obtainable at most fashionable English hotels. At the Carlton it is generally made in an infuser tea pot.'

Mrs CF Leyel, *The General Art of Cooking*, 1925

There are three distinct varieties: the annual GERMAN CHAMOMILE (*Matricaria recutita*); the perennial ROMAN CHAMOMILE (*Chamaemelum nobile*); and the non-flowering TRENEAGUE. **Family:** *Asteraceae* (*Compositae*)

GERMAN CHAMOMILE (*Matricaria recutita*)
Type: HA   **Height:** 30cm (1ft)
Position preferred: prefers sun. Will grow in poor sandy soils.
When and how to sow: sow in April in shallow drills 30cm (1ft) apart just covering the seed. Thin to 15cm (6in) apart.
When and how to propagate: by seeds only.
Leaf and flower colour and time of flowering: growing season is quite short. Seed sown in April will be flowering and ready to harvest in June/July. German chamomile is erect-growing and produces many branches. Leaves are feathery and grey-green. The whole plant smells of pineapple.
Main usefulness: chamomile tea is an ideal family remedy for restlessness and irritability. Chamomile is a mild sedative, good at bedtime, or in cases of children's travel sickness. Chamomile tastes bitter. A spoonful of honey will improve the taste.
Other virtues: chamomile is regarded as anti-inflammatory, antiseptic and antifungal. Some American herb growers use cold chamomile tea as a spray to prevent 'damping-off' of seedlings. Use an infusion of the flowers as a natural hair rinse for fair hair.
How to keep for later use: pick the flowers when in full bloom, dry and store.
ROMAN CHAMOMILE (*Chamaemelum nobile* formerly *Anthemis nobilis*)

Type: HP   **Height:** 30cm (1ft)
Position preferred: full sun in well-drained soils.
When and how to sow: sow in seed trays, especially if your plants are to form a chamomile lawn. Do not cover seed but press gently into the compost. Sow March–May.
When and how to propagate: Roman chamomile produces side shoots. Lifted in March–April, these will root readily out of doors. Side shoots can be lifted during the summer and rooted in the same way as cuttings; or put directly into small pots and kept well-watered. Plant 45cm (18in) apart in rows 60cm (2ft) apart. When grown as a crop, Roman chamomile beds are lifted every three years.
Leaf and flower colour and time of flowering: leaves are feathery and bright green. Flowers are white-petalled with a yellow centre like a daisy, produced from July to September. Commercial growers pick the flower heads up to five times a season. There is a double flowered variety.
Main usefulness: home remedy uses are as German chamomile. Roman chamomile is the chamomile from which scented lawns can be made. Plant 30cm (1ft) apart in all directions in well-drained soil and water well. When plants show new growth, roll. You will need to hand-weed during the first year until the plants grow to exclude competitive weeds. Hand clip your chamomile lawn to prevent the flower heads forming. You may also make chamomile 'seats' (a raised bed the length of a bench) in the same way.
Other virtues: as German chamomile.
How to keep for later use: as German chamomile.
Non-flowering variety: TRENEAGUE is the non-flowering form. Plant about 22.5cm (9in) for a full lawn. Treneague does not look as attractive as Roman chamomile during the winter since it dies down and exposes the soil.

CHERVIL

'This salad is much preferr'd for its fine biting taste, before many other dull herbs.'
                                    John Worlidge, *The Art of Gardening*, 1688.

Botanical name: *Anthriscus cerefolium*   **Family:** *Apiaceae (Umbelliferae)*
Type: HA   **Height:** 50cm (1ft 8in)
Position preferred: cool and shady or part-shady.
When and how to sow: from February to April in a moist bed with some shade. Chervil will quickly run to seed under hot, dry conditions. Sow in winter for use late summer in a sunny, open border since at this time of the year chervil needs more light. Chervil does not transplant well. Plants should be thinned to 15cm (6in) apart.
When and how to propagate: by seed only.

Leaf and flower colour and time of flowering: small feathery green leaves. Small white flowers in umbels.

Main usefulness: with basil, chives and tarragon, an ingredient of *fines herbes*, a blend of herbs widely used in French cooking. Chervil leaves have an anise-like parsley flavour. Delicious with egg dishes, sauces, salads.

Other virtues: regarded as a diuretic and stimulant. Has been used to lower blood pressure.

How to keep for later use: cut leaves eight to twelve weeks after sowing. Dry with care to preserve flavour.

CHICORY

Botanical name: *Cichorium intybus*   **Family:** *Asteracaea (Compositae)*
Type: HP   **Height:** 1m (3ft 4in)
Position preferred: well drained, limed soils in good heart.
When and how to sow: sow seed 3mm (⅛in) deep April–May, earlier if sown in seed trays. Transplant 30cm (1ft) apart.
When and how to propagate: by seeds only.
Leaf and flower colour and time of flowering: leaves are light green. Bright blue flowers on long upright formal stems from July to September. New flowers appear daily, opening early in the morning and closing in the early afternoon.
Main usefulness: chicory leaves are forced and blanched by putting a bucket or large plant pot over the plants in spring. Chicory roots are dried and ground for use as a coffee substitute.
Other virtues: chicory root is considered an aid to digestion. The French believe its addition to coffee 'buffers' the coffee, making it more digestible.
How to keep for later use: the roots with their crowns can be lifted in October and stored until the winter. They are subsequently placed in boxes and pots and brought into a warm dark place. This will produce long, white leaves for winter salads within two to four weeks. Roots are dried, cut into small pieces, roasted and ground.

CHIVES

Botanical name: *Allium schoenoprasum*   **Family:** *Liliaceae*
Type: HP   **Height:** 15cm (6in)
Position preferred: chives enjoy a moist well-worked soil with plenty of humus. Chives will grow in some shade. Chives make a neat and colourful edging to a border. Chives will grow in tubs, window boxes and pots. For convenience, plant chives as close to the kitchen as possible since they are always in need.

When and how to sow: in the spring or autumn, sow 1.5cm (½in) apart in seed boxes or outside in drills. Germination under glass at 70°F is six days. Outside, germination will be fourteen days plus. Thin or transplant to 15cm (6in) apart. A chive seedling produces a thin, tapering green shoot from an elongated white bulb. Since chives grow by their small bulbs producing new bulbs, you can transplant several seedlings as a 'bunch' without fear of overcrowding.

When and how to propagate: established clumps can be lifted in the spring, autumn and even the summer if the weather is damp, and divided by pulling into smaller clumps. Always water well after replanting, and trim the tops to encourage new growth of the leaves. Chives soon exhaust the soil so feeding is essential where chives have been planted in containers. Chives need watering in dry weather. Lift chives every three years, divide the clumps and replant in fresh soil.

Leaf and flower colour and time of flowering: chives produce green, tubular leaves that look rather like grass. It is these leaves which are cut about 1.5cm (½in) above the ground for culinary use. Chives produce round, pinky-mauve flowers rather like thrift. Seeds turn black when ripe.

Main usefulness: chives are as indispensable as parsley in any kitchen. Chives add a delicate, appetising mild onion flavour. Chives are generally chopped and sprinkled on salads, soups, scrambled eggs, omelettes, mashed potatoes; mixed in cottage and cream cheese and dips. Chives make an attractive garnish. Chives are one of the four herbs in the French *fines herbes* mixture.

Other virtues: chives have the reputation of improving the appetite. The flower heads can be dried for winter flower arrangements.

How to keep for later use: chives freeze very well either chopped or just as cut. Frozen chives can be cut and chopped without thawing.

Other varieties:

GIANT CHIVES (*Allium schoenophrasum* var. *sibiricum*) are a larger form of chives, flowers reaching 30cm (1ft) in height. Taste and uses are identical to the smaller form although the leaves are coarser and thicker.

GARLIC or **ORIENTAL CHIVES** (*Allium tuberosum*) are used to impart a delicate garlic flavour and are widely used in oriental cooking both as a vegetable and to flavour. Flowers are white.

COLTSFOOT

Botanical name: *Tussilago farfara*   **Family:** *Asteraceae (Compositae)*
Type: HP   **Height:** 20cm (8in)
Position preferred: any soil.
When and how to sow: the seeds have their own downy parachutes.

These need anchoring in a seed tray by covering with fine sand. Sow early spring and transplant when large enough to handle. Coltsfoot disappears completely during the winter so you will need to mark where you have planted the seedlings. Coltsfoot can be invasive. It is an ideal herb for a piece of waste land.

When and how to propagate: pieces of root will transplant easily almost anytime if kept moist after replanting.

Leaf and flower colour and time of flowering: coltsfoot was once called *filius ante patrem* (the son before the father) because the flowers appear before the leaves. Single bright yellow flowers similar to dandelions appear in February and March. Green veined heart-shaped leaves appear later and grow larger throughout the summer.

Main usefulness: a decoction of the dried leaves is used in cases of persistent bronchial cough. Coltsfoot is an expectorant and helps stop irritation.

Other virtues: its yellow flowers are a very welcome early reminder of the spring.

How to keep for later use: pick and dry the leaves in June and early July.

COMFREY

'Every member of the Borage family is useful medicinally, but the Comfrey surpasses them all as the best established vulnerary. It heals internally and externally. For diseased bones and diseased lungs, it has no equal.'

Mrs CF Leyel, *Compassionate Herbs*, 1946.

Botanical name: *Symphytum officinale*　　**Family:** *Boraginaceae*
Type: HP　　**Height:** 120cm (47in)
Position preferred: sun or semi-shade with plenty of moisture.
When and how to sow: sow early spring either where it is to flower or in trays for later planting. Sow in shallow drills.
When and how to propagate: division of established plants in spring and autumn. Lift and split roots in the winter.
Leaf and flower colour and time of flowering: coarse, hairy, large green leaves. Drooping white or mauve flowers like small bells.
Main usefulness: comfrey leaf is used in cases of gastric and duodenal ulcer, rheumatic pain and arthritis. As a poultice, it is used in bruises and sprains. Comfrey root is helpful in cases of colitis.
Other virtues: horses and cattle adore eating comfrey. They will break down fences to reach it. It is used by several successful race horse trainers.
How to keep for later use: gather the leaves from May onwards. Dry leaves separately otherwise they will turn black. Dig up the brownish-black root in the autumn, wash and dry.

Comfrey

Coriander and costmary

Dandelion and dill

Other varieties:
RUSSIAN COMFREY (*Symphytum uplandicum* formerly *symphytum peregrinum*) has clear pale blue flowers and grows to 2m (6ft 8in). *Symphytum caucasicum* has early gentian blue flowers and grows to 1m (3ft 4in) high. Both are excellent ornamental plants for the herb garden.
CREEPING COMFREY (*Symphytum grandiflorum*) grows to 13cm (5in) and produces creamy yellow drooping flowers early in the spring and again in the autumn. Useful ground cover plant under trees. Valuable source of early nectar for bees.

Before planting any comfrey, make sure you are happy with its position. It is a difficult plant to eradicate once established.

CORIANDER

'The leaves of Coriander have a strong disagreeable scent. The seeds are grateful to the taste and are sold by confectioners, incrusted with sugar.'

Thomas Martyn, *Flora Russica*, 1792

Botanical name: *Coriandrum sativum*   **Family:** *Apiaceae (Umbelliereae)*
Type: HA   **Height:** 60cm (2ft)
Position preferred: open, sunny situation with good, moisture-retentive soil.
When and how to sow: can be sown in seed boxes and transplanted but ideal to sow outside in April and successively throughout the summer. Coriander will produce leaves until the first frosts. Sow 6mm (¼in) deep in double rows 15cm (6in) apart and thin to 15cm (6in) between the plants. Allow 30cm (1ft) between each double row. Germination is quick.
When and how to propagate: by seed only.
Leaf and flower colour and time of flowering: leaves are shiny bright green. Flowers are pale mauve produced in umbels in July and August. The whole plant has a smell of rancid fat, some say of bugs. The large round waxy seeds (botanically called 'fruits') also have this disagreeable smell until they are ripe. The seeds, then beige in colour with a thin paper-like covering, develop a pleasant aromatic smell reminiscent of honey and oranges.
Main usefulness: ground coriander seeds are a staple ingredient of many curry powders. Whole seeds are added to pickles and chutneys. Fresh coriander leaves (*hara dhania* in Hindi) are used to flavour particularly lentil (*dhal*) dishes when they are added towards the end of cooking. Fresh leaves are also used for garnishing in Indian cookery.
Other virtues: coriander seeds are still candied for cake decorations. In the seventeenth century, coriander 'comfits' were a popular after-dinner sweetmeat which were eaten liberally to aid digestion and ease wind.

How to keep for later use: when the first seeds are ripe, cut down the plant and dry in a warm place. Rub the dry ripe seeds off the remains of the plant and store in a closed container in a dry place. Coriander leaves do not freeze. Fresh leaves can be kept in oil or vinegar for winter use.

Costmary

'The flowers are tyed up with small bundels of Lavender toppes, these being put in the middle of them, to lye upon the toppes of beds, presses etc. for the sweete sent and flavour it causeth.'

John Parkinson, *Paradisi in Sole*, 1629

Botanical name: *Chysanthemum balsamita* formerly *Tanacetum balsamita*
Family: *Asteraceae (Compositae)*
Type: HP   **Height:** 150–180cm (5–6ft)
Position preferred: any soil in dry, sunny position. Costmary is a lanky, rather untidy large plant so allow plenty of room: about 4ft between costmary and its neighbours.
When and how to sow: in the spring in open ground or seed boxes. Seeds are difficult to obtain.
When and how to propagate: lift an established clump in the spring/late autumn and divide the roots.
Leaf and flower colour and time of flowering: the popular American name for costmary is Bible Leaf, a reference to the time when the large serrated-edged leaves (up to 15cm (6in) long and 3.5cm (1½in) wide) carried on long stalks were used as a natural book mark for a bible. Flowers are produced in August: yellow flowers like small daisies with a yellow centre produced in clusters.
Main usefulness: the leaves give a mild minty flavour to soups and stews. Dry the leaves and flowers for use in pot-pourri. Use crushed leaves in moth mixtures with tansy, southernwood, wormwood and lavender.
Other virtues: historically, costmary was thought to be good for the liver and to strengthen the stomach. The leaves were used to flavour ale – hence its other name ALECOST. An infusion of costmary was used to wash the hair to take away scurf.
How to keep for later use: strip the leaves from their stems. Dry in the normal way.

Cowslip

'The cowslips tall her pensioners be;
In their gold coats spots you see;
Those be rubies, fairy favours,
In those freckles live their savours.'

William Shakespeare, *A Midsummer Night's Dream*

Botanical name: *Primula veris*   **Family:** *Primulaceae*

Garlic and elderflower

Type: HP **Height:** 30cm (1ft)

Position preferred: full sun in meadows, on banks, against walls.

When and how to sow: seeds should be sown in the autumn. Cowslip seeds need a period of cold weather before they will germinate. If you sow later, ie in the spring, putting your seed tray in the refrigerator for about 3 weeks will have the same effect. Seedlings are very tiny and need transplanting soon after the true leaves form. It is noticeable that seedlings make the most of their growth early in the spring so if you delay transplanting you will end up with smaller plants the following spring. It is wise not to sow too thickly.

When and how to propagate: cowslips do not like disturbance of the roots but it is possible to separate mature plants in the spring and autumn.

Leaf and flower colour and time of flowering: bright green leaves that grow larger after the herb flowers. Bright yellow bell-shaped flowers on stiff stems above the rosette of leaves. Attractive to bees.

Main usefulness: cowslips are sedative. A tea of cowslips taken in the evening is relaxing and encourages sleep. Cowslip tea may make you dream since cowslips are slightly narcotic. Cowslip tea tastes pleasantly of honey.

Other virtues: cowslip flowers can be made into jellies, wine and used in salads. Use only flowers from your own garden since cowslips in the wild are becoming increasingly rare.

How to keep for later use: cut the flower heads when fully open in April–May. Dry the flower heads thoroughly. Culpeper advised 'keep a

Feverfew

special eye on them. If you let them see the sun once a Month, it will do neither the Sun nor them harm'. Giving them an airing in this way helps prevent the dried flower heads going brown. Flowers can be frozen.

CUMIN

'If anyone that hath eaten Cuminseeds, do breathe on a painted face, the fictitious colour will vanish away straight.'

William Coles, *Adam in Eden*, 1657

Botanical name: *Cuminum cyminum*   **Family:** *Apiaceae (Umbelliferae)*
Type: HHA   **Height:** 15cm (6in)
Position preferred: well drained, rich, sandy soils, preferably sheltered. Cumin is native to the Mediterranean and will not grow much below 50°F. Cumin grows best in mild temperatures during its twelve to sixteen week growing period.
When and how to sow: outdoors in May where the plants are to grow. Sow in drills ¼in deep, thin to 10cm (4in) apart. Seeds can be started earlier under glass. Individual sowing into compartmentalised trays makes transplanting easier since the seedlings may be pushed out from the bottom with their root ball intact. Cumin is a rather frail, tender plant and needs careful handling.
When and how to propagate: by seed only.
Leaf and flower colour and time of flowering: deep green divided leaves similar to fennel but much smaller. White or whitish-pink flowers in umbels (ie a flower like an umbrella, each flower on its own stalk radiating out from a central stem) appear June-July. Seeds ripen July-August and are ripe when they change colour.
Main usefulness: cumin is used mainly as an ingredient of curry powders; and as a flavouring agent in cheeses, biscuits, pickles and soups.
Other virtues: cumin was regarded by early herbalists as one of the 'foure great Carminative-seeds, and therfore it dissolveth Wind in any part of the body'.
How to keep for later use: take up the whole plant when the seeds first change colour. Dry in an airy place. Rub off dry seeds. Store in a cool, dry place.

DANDELION

'Dandelyon, vulgarly called, Piss-a-beds.'

Nicholas Culpeper, *English Physician*, 1652

Botanical name: *Taraxum officinale*   **Family:** *Asteraceae (Compositae)*
Type: HP   **Height:** 30cm (1ft)
Position preferred: dandelion will grow virtually anywhere but if cultivated, choose a well-worked soil free of recent manuring.

When and how to sow: the seeds each have their own 'parachute' so sow in drills 1.2cm (½in) deep in April. Thin to 15cm (6in) apart. If growing for leaves, keep removing the flower heads.

When and how to propagate: dandelion is difficult to eradicate. Any small piece of root will form a plant.

Leaf and flower colour and time of flowering: the leaves are grouped in a rosette around the crown of the roots, dark green, 'deeply gashed' and spread along the ground. The bright yellow flowers appear on upright stems as early as February. Flowers are a valuable source of pollen for the early bee.

Main usefulness: tender young leaves are used in salads. The taste is bitter and stimulating. Blanched leaves can be produced throughout the winter to use in winter salads. A wine can be made from the flowers and leaves. The roots are dried and ground for use as a non-caffeinated coffee substitute.

Other virtues: dandelion is diuretic hence its 'vulgar' reputation. The herb is also laxative. Dandelion root and leaf (the root is stronger) are used by herbalists to treat muscular rheumatism, gall-stones and jaundice. Dandelion is thought to help in detoxifying the body.

How to keep for later use: gather the leaves for drying before the flowers bloom in May. A second harvest can be made in September. Dig up the roots in autumn or spring, remove the leafy tops, thoroughly wash and dry. Use only the thin roots.

To produce blanched leaves during the winter, roots are lifted in November and stored in damp sand in a cool dark place. At intervals, roots are placed close together in moist soil in large pots which are then placed in a warm environment. The pots are kept either in the dark or covered to exclude the light. Using this method, it is possible to have fresh leaves from November to April when the roots are thrown away.

DILL

'It is put among pickled cowcumbers wherwith it doth very well agree.'

John Parkinson, *Paradisi in Sole,* 1629

Botanical name: *Anethum graveolens* also *Peucedanum graveolens*
Family: *Apiaceae (Umbelliferae)*
Type: HA **Height:** 1m (3ft 4in)
Position preferred: rich deep soil in sheltered location. Dill grows well in cool conditions.
When and how to sow: William Coles (1657) called dill 'a wise plant, not being willing to venture abroad, till the winter be gone'. Sow in April in open ground in shallow drills. If growing for leaves, do not thin

Fennel

Horseradish

Heartsease

'Cats are very much delighted' with all species of catmint

but sow thinly and allow about 45cm (18in) between rows. If sowing for flowers, allow about 30cm (1ft) between each plant. Sowing in seed trays under glass can start in March. Transplant seedlings to small pots for growing on, transplanting later to where they are to flower.

When and how to propagate: by seed only.

Leaf and flower colour and time of flowering: foliage is feathery and blue-green. Flowers are yellow in umbels on hollow stems.

Main usefulness: fresh dill herb (sometimes called dill weed) and fresh flowers are used to garnish salmon and other fish dishes. Chop dill leaves and mix in salads. Dill is widely used in Scandinavia with new potatoes and as a garnish. Dill adds a smooth, warm flavour to fish, of which it helps the digestion. Both the seeds and herb can be used to flavour vinegars, pickled gherkins and cucumbers. Try chopped dill with cucumber sandwiches, on scrambled eggs and mashed potatoes.

Other virtues: dill is carminative. An infusion of the seeds is used to treat flatulent dyspepsia and the gripes. It is an ingredient in gripe water; and is believed to stimulate the production of breast milk in humans.

How to keep for later use: harvest seeds as for caraway. Pickle both ripe fresh seeds and leaves in vinegar. Dry flower heads and stalks for winter flower arrangements. Freeze flower heads and leaves. Preserve the herb and flower heads in oil.

Varieties: because of the wide demand for fresh dill in America, there are two good named varieties, unusual for a herb:

BOUQUET is a vigorous, upright variety that produces plenty of branches and compact heads of flowers. Grows to 91cm (3ft).

DUKAT is a taller plant than Bouquet with larger flower heads. Grows to 1.06m (3ft 6in).

ECHINACEA

North American plant commonly called Coneflower.

Botanical name: *Echinacea angustifolia* **Family:** *Asteraceae (Compositae)*

Type: HP   **Height:** 60cm (2ft)

Position preferred: well-drained sunny position in deep, rich soil.

When and how to sow: germination is uneven so it is best to sow in seed trays. Sow 3mm (⅛in) deep in temperature about 55°F. Plant out about 45cm (18in) apart when large enough.

When and how to propagate: established plants can be divided in October and March–April.

Leaf and flower colour and time of flowering: leaves are long, pointed, dark green. The flowers which appear in August are up to 15cm (6in) across, with a dark domed centre and daisy-like purple flower petals.

Main usefulness: echinacea root is used in infusion or decoction to treat boils, carbuncles and abscesses. It is thus a useful herb to help clear up general poor skin conditions.

Other virtues: modern research interest in echinacea centres around its antiviral properties and the indication that the herb strengthens the body's immune system. Echinacea was used by the North American Souix Indian against septicaemia and infection.

How to keep for later use: roots are lifted in the autumn, washed and dried.

ELDER

'In the tops of the branches and twigs, there spingeth sweet and crisped umbels, swelling with white sweet-smelling flowers (in June before St John's Eve) which by their fall, give place to a many branched Grape, first green, then ruddy, lastly of a black, dark purple-colour, succulent and tumid with its winish liquor.'

Dr Martin Blochwich, *The Anatomie of the Elder*, 1670

Botanical name: *Sambucus nigra*   **Family:** *Caprifoliaceae*
Type: Hardy shrub   **Height:** 6m (20ft)
Position preferred: elderflower will grow anywhere in sun or part-shade.
When and how to sow: sow the dried berries 12mm (½in) deep outdoors in the spring in a seed bed. Transplant to where you want them to grow in the autumn. Bushes take up to five years to bear flowers.
When and how to propagate: take 15cm (6in) cuttings in October to March and insert in moist ground outside. You can also take stem cuttings of fresh young growth early in the spring.
Leaf and flower colour and time of flowering: feather-shaped green leaves appear very early in the year. Whole plant has disagreeable smell. Flowers are born in rich creamy umbels in June.
Main usefulness: elderflowers make a delicious syrup, wine and jelly, with a taste rather like lychees. The syrup can be used to flavour gooseberries, fresh fruit salads, ice-cream; and drunk hot or cold in dilution. The wine is often made in a sparkling form. Elderflower jelly goes well with game, lamb and poultry. Elderberries can be made into wine and jam.
Other virtues: an infusion of elderflowers promotes perspiration and is anticatarrhal. Elderflowers are thus a useful home remedy in the treatment of colds, influenza and sinusitis. Peppermint, hyssop and yarrow combine well with elderflower.
How to keep for later use: pick the flower heads when in full bloom and covered in pollen. Place the heads upside down on paper or an old sheet. When dry, rub the flowers away from the stalks. The berries should be picked when ripe and dried to the consistency of a currant. Flowers can be frozen.

A border of lavender and hyssop

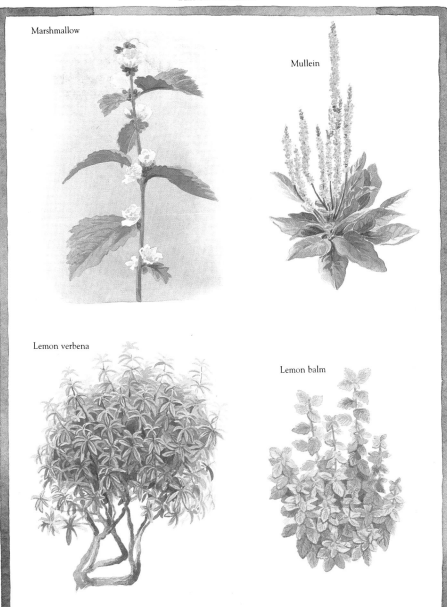

Marshmallow

Mullein

Lemon verbena

Lemon balm

FENNEL

Botanical name: *Foeniculum vulgare*   **Family:** *Apiaceae (Umbelliferae)*
Type: HP   **Height:** 1.5–1.8m (5–6ft)
Position preferred: open sunny situation in good, moist soil.
When and how to sow: sow outside April/May, a month earlier if under glass. Sow 6mm (¼in) deep in drills. Transplant or thin to 30cm (1ft) apart. If growing fennel in rows, allow 37.5cm (15in) between the rows.
When and how to propagate: divide clumps every few years in March, replant side shoots and rooted pieces, then water well.
Leaf and flower colour and time of flowering: green feathery fronds with large umbels of yellow flowers August–September.
Main usefulness: fennel has a pleasant sweet aniseed flavour that is retained whether fresh, dried or in seed form. The fresh fronds are added to salads, peas, beans, fish and poultry either chopped or used decoratively. The fronds and slices of the bulb variety Florence fennel or *Finocchio* (see variety below) can be used to put in dips or eaten as 'ante-pasta'. Fish and poultry cooked with fennel have a wonderful flavour.
Other virtues: fennel is an important medical herb listed in the *British Herbal Pharmacopaeia*. Medicinally, the fruits (commonly called seeds) are used since these contain a greater concentration of the plant's volatile oils. Fennel is used in cases of flatulent dyspepsia, and flatulent colic in children. If you study the formula on a well known gripe water, you will find the formula includes fennel as well as dill. Fennel is orexigenic, ie stimulates the appetite, and is used by herbalists to treat anorexia. Conversely, 'both Leaves, Seeds and Roots hereof are much used in Drinks or Broths, to make people more spare and lean that are too fat'[1] – a recognition of fennel's diuretic properties. Fennel is anti-inflammatory and anti-microbial, hence its use as a gargle and eye-wash. Fennel has the reputation of stimulating breast milk production, a view shared in Chinese medicine. And the milk so produced will of course contain some of fennel's carminative properties.
How to keep for later use: save the seeds when ripe. Dry and store in a cool, airtight container when dry. Cut the whole stalks to just above the ground. Tie in bunches and dry in an airing cupboard or hang in a warm greenhouse or airy shed. Cut the dried stems to a useful size to use in the kitchen. Store in bundles in a dry place or freeze leaves.
Varieties:
BRONZE FENNEL A more decorative version as fully at home in the flower border as in the herb or vegetable garden. Particularly beautiful

[1]Nicholas Culpeper, *The English Physician*, 1652

towards the end of August when the unopened flower heads carry the bronze tint of the foliage. Grow and treat as common fennel.

FLORENCE FENNEL (FINOCCHIO) (*Foeniculum dulce*) is grown as an annual to produce the white 'bulb' (in fact, the blanched swollen bases of the leaf stalks) which is eaten as a vegetable, cooked and raw. Sow Florence fennel in drills 45cm (18in) apart and thin the seedlings to one every 15cm (6in). Earth the plants up on either side of the row as the bulb begins to form. Feed regularly and grow in a warm sunny spot that has plenty of moisture. Do not allow to flower.

FEVERFEW

Botanical name: *Tanacetum parthenium* formerly *Chrysanthemum parthenium*   **Family:** *Asteraceae (Compositae)*

Type: HP   **Height:** 45cm (18in)

Position preferred: well-drained soil with sunny aspect.

When and how to sow: sow seed in seedboxes from March onwards under cover. Press seed in or just cover with a sieve. Sow outside April onwards in shallow drills. Plants should be thinned to 30cm (1ft) apart.

When and how to propagate: stem cuttings can be taken throughout the year. Cuttings will root more readily in the spring.

Leaf and flower colour and time of flowering: leaves are yellowy-green, deeply segmented and aromatic when crushed. Flowers are white petalled with yellow centres like daisies produced in flat-topped clusters from July to October. There is a double flowered variety and a pretty golden feverfew (var. *Aureum*) whose leaves are a deep yellow.

Main usefulness: modern research has proved that feverfew helps prevent painful migraine attacks. There is also evidence that feverfew helps headaches caused by nervous tension and has some value in arthritis. Two to three fresh leaves eaten every day are a preventative.

Other virtues: leaves can be dried and used in moth mixtures.

How to keep for later use: gather the whole plant, leaves and flowers and dry in June/July. Pot plants in the autumn to overwinter in the greenhouse or conservatory if you need fresh leaves for migraine prevention. Leaves may be frozen.

GARLIC

'It is a tribute to the stubbornness of English conservatism that, in two books on herbs published within the last twelve years, no mention is made in one of them of any culinary uses of Garlic at all, while the other states briefly that in this country Garlic is not appreciated.'

Ambrose Heath, *Herbs in the Kitchen*, 1953

Marigolds and lovage

Marjoram: *(clockwise)* golden, wild, pot, sweet, winter

Botanical name: *Allium sativum*   **Family:** *Liliaceae*
Type: HP   **Height:** 30–90cm (1–3ft)
Position preferred: fertile, well drained soil in sunny position.
When and how to sow: 'sowing' in the case of garlic consists of planting the cloves which are split from the garlic bulb. If you pick up a whole garlic bulb, you can feel the outline of the cloves under the skin. Split the cloves away from the bulb but do not damage the cloves in doing this. The cloves should be planted 5cm (2in) deep, 15cm (6in) apart in rows 30cm (1ft) apart. Planting can be done at any time during the autumn/early winter, and again in the spring. Bulbs planted in the autumn tend to be bigger. Depending on the weather, your garlic clove will send up a flat, bright green shoot. No further care is necessary except keeping the plants free of weeds. In August the leaves will turn brown and start to wither. You should now lift your garlic for drying. Get a fork underneath the bulbs – remember you planted the cloves 5cm deep so push your fork into the ground about 7cm (3in) away from the row and well under the depth of the bulb. In this way, you will not stick the prongs of the fork through the bulb nor damage it. If the weather is fine and sunny, lay your bulbs with their drying leaves on the ground so that the soil around the roots can dry. If wet, put the bulbs under cover, somewhere where there is a good current of air. A good way to dry garlic bulbs is to make a frame of wire netting 30cm (1ft) or more above the ground (the ever useful orange box makes a good base) and spread the bulbs complete with their roots and leaves on the frame until the leaves and the soil around the roots are thoroughly dry. At this point, you can rub away the roots with the soil from the base and cut off the withered leaves about 3cm (1in) above the top of the bulb. If you attempt to do this before the roots and tops are dry, you will damage the bulb which will then not keep well. At all times, handle garlic bulbs carefully to avoid bruising.
　　If at any time during the growing period, your garlic attempts to flower, nip the flower bud off as soon as you see it – you want the plant's energy to go into making a large bulb, not in producing flowers. The flower bud appears between the leaves on the tip of a quick-growing single firm stem.
When and how to propagate: see above.
Leaf and flower colour and time of flowering: garlic leaves are flat (like leek leaves) and dark green. Garlic flowers are white.
Main usefulness: if you love your food, garlic is an essential ingredient in your kitchen. If you are growing your own garlic, a real luxury is to lift some of the immature bulbs during the summer and chop for use in salads. Always cook lamb studded with garlic cloves cut in slices. Add

garlic to all soups, stuffings, pasta and pizzas. You cannot have enough garlic. Garlic encourages the appetite and is good for the stomach. If you are worried about the effect on your breath, take heart that millions of people eat garlic regularly. If you are really worried, chew some fresh parsley. To get the smell off your fingers, rub these with a cut lemon. And parsley and lemon go very well with garlic in your cooking.

Other virtues: if your family eat garlic regularly (particularly raw, as crushed into salad dressings), it is unlikely that they will come down with colds – nor are your family likely to develop thread or other worms. Garlic is antiseptic, antiviral and antibacterial. Garlic (like onions) helps to reduce high blood pressure. Allicin, an active compound of garlic, has been shown to inhibit tumour growth.

Only small diluted doses of raw garlic should be fed to small children.

How to keep for later use: store the dried bulbs in a string, their dried leaves being plaited. Store garlic cloves in a garlic cellar, an earthenware vessel with holes in the side that permit the free circulation of air. Garlic kept like this will last well into the spring.

Varieties

ELEPHANT or **GREAT-HEADED GARLIC** (*Allium ampeloprasum*). Grows to 150cm (5ft) and produces large, heavy bulbs which can be ⅓ kilo (12oz) each in weight. Cultivation is similar to ordinary garlic except that the bulbs are planted with their tops just below well worked soil. The soil is then trenched on either side of the row in the same way as potatoes are earthed up. This creates an easy environment in which the bulb can grow and expand. Elephant garlic is milder in taste.

GARLIC CHIVES *see* **CHIVES**

SCENTED GERANIUM

Botanical name: *Pelargonium graveolens* and species
Family: *Geraniaceae*
Type: HHP **Height:** to 1m (3ft 4in)
Position preferred: sunny, well-drained soils. In temperate climates scented geraniums are normally grown in pots since they need some heat in winter as they are *not* frost hardy. Scented geraniums originated in South Africa. They do not like being given little drops of water now and then, but prefer a thorough soak when their soil is completely dry. Scented geraniums respond to feeding.

When and how to sow: seeds can sometimes be obtained commercially. It is worth saving seed from your own plants. Sow in trays individually 12mm (½in) deep at 70°F.

When and how to propagate: stem cuttings can be taken anytime where your plants are protected. Geranium cuttings are judged to strike better if they are 'cured', ie left some hours before they are inserted in the cutting compost. Strong side shoots are chosen up to 4in in length. Geranium cuttings need bottom heat in winter and spring if they are to produce roots. Scented geraniums root best in a 50/50 mixture of Perlite and peat.

Leaf and flower colour and time of flowering: leaves are serrated, fragrant, deeply lobed, their size depending on variety. Some plants have sticky leaves. Flowers vary in colour from white to shades of red, violet, mauve but all are small to insignificant.

Main usefulness: scented geraniums are grown commercially overseas for distillation of their essential oil. The oil is used in perfumes, cosmetics and toiletries. Scented geranium leaves can be used to flavour fruit salads, puddings and custards to which they add a rose fragrance. Dried leaves are used in sachets and pot-pourri. Scented geraniums make an excellent house plant giving rooms a delightful spicy fragrance.

Other virtues: Mrs Grieve in *A Modern Herbal* (1932) writes that most scented geraniums are astringent and have value in dysentry and ulcers but there appears to be no other confirmation from any other source of these particular properties.

How to keep for later use: pot and bring all plants indoors for the winter. Scented geraniums need plenty of light. Water only when you see the leaves begin to droop. Dry the leaves for use in sachets and pot-pourri.

A good variety to grow: *P. graveolens*

HEARTSEASE

Botanical name: *Viola tricolor*   **Family:** *Violaceae*
Type: HA   **Height:** 20cm (8in)
Position preferred: any good garden soil in full sun.
When and how to sow: sow in March–May 6mm (¼in) deep where they are to flower or preferably in seed trays. Thin or transplant to 22.5cm (9in) apart.
When and how to propagate: by seed only is normal although it is possible to take cuttings which will root easily.
Flower colour and time of flowering: flowers are three coloured: purple, yellow and white, produced in great abundance on many-branching stems. Attractive to bees and butterflies.
Main usefulness: fast-growing, very colourful carpet to the herb garden, useful to fill formal arrangements. Flowers are sweetly scented and can be added to salads and summer wine cups. Flowers can be dried and added to pot-pourri. Press flowers for floral greetings cards.
Other virtues: heartsease is laxative, diuretic and antirheumatic. An

infusion of the leaves and flowers is used to treat cases of eczema, bronchitis and cystitis.

How to keep for later use: collect the leaves and flowers May–August and dry.

HOREHOUND

'In Norfolk scarcely a cottage garden can be found without its Horehound corner, and Horehound beer is commonly drunk there by the natives.'

Dr WT Fernie, *Meals Medicinal*, 1905

Botanical name: *Marrubium vulgare*   **Family:** *Lamiaceae (Labiatae)*

Type: HP   **Height:** 60cm (2ft)

Position preferred: will grow in poor, dry soil.

When and how to sow: sow seed in April in shallow drills and transplant to 25cm (10in) apart.

When and how to propagate: plants can be divided in March. Cuttings can be taken during the summer.

Flower colour and time of flowering: small white flowers are produced in whorls along erect stems. Flowers are attractive to bees.

Main usefulness: the leaves and flowering tops are used in infusion for the treatment of bronchitis and whooping cough. Horehound is in the *British Herbal Pharmacopaeia* and was for many years in the official British pharmacopaeias until superceded by synthetic drugs.

Other virtues: because of its medicinal properties, candied horehound was a popular winter sweetmeat.

How to keep for later use: dry the whole plant while it is in flower June–September.

HORSERADISH

Botanical name: *Armoracia rusticana*   **Family:** *Brassicaceae (Cruciferae)*

Type: HP   **Height:** 1m (3ft 4in)

Position preferred: deep, damp, light soil rich in organic matter. Because horseradish is difficult to extirpate once established, you will prefer to plant in a part of the garden where it will not disturb other plants. Planting in light soil makes harvesting much easier. Liberal addition of organic manure before planting produces the finest roots.

When and how to sow: horseradish is generally considered to be sterile. Seed is thus unobtainable.

When and how to propagate: root cuttings and root crowns (a piece of root of which the top is enlarged and bears the marks of fallen leaves) about 30cm (12in) long are planted a foot apart in prepared ground. The cuttings are planted upright (remember to plant the crown on top!) in holes made with a dibber 30–37cm (12–15in) deep. All side shoots should be removed from the cuttings before planting. Fill the holes containing the horseradish roots with a little fine soil. Water well.

Planting can be done in November or January/February. The cuttings will grow in width but not in length until the end of the growing season in October/November.

Leaf and flower colour and time of flowering: the main leaves are long and broad with serrated edges. Lower leaves are heavily toothed. The leaves are regarded as poisonous to both humans and cattle. Flowers are white with purplish sepals and appear May–June.

Main usefulness: horseradish sauce is the traditional accompaniment to roast beef. Horseradish sauce is also good with fish and seafood.

Other virtues: horseradish is considered a stimulant, good for the stomach, and a diuretic.

How to keep for later use: lift the roots in October/November and store. Roots may be stored in a cool place in the dark; grated and frozen or grated and kept in vinegar.

Warning: it is suggested that you should never plant horseradish anywhere near Aconite since the roots have been confused with fatal effects.

HYSSOP

Botanical name: *Hyssopus officinalis*   **Family:** *Lamiaceae (Labiatae)*
Type: HP   **Height:** 60cm (2ft)

Position preferred: sunny, well-drained soils. Will stand partial shade.

When and how to sow: seeds can be sown in open ground in drills about 6mm (¼in) deep or in seed trays and transplanted. Plants should be thinned or transplanted to 30cm (1ft) apart. Hyssop makes a good hedge when plants are spaced about 23cm (9in) apart.

When and how to propagate: cuttings about 5cm (2in) long of non-flowering shoots taken in the summer will root within fourteen days.

Leaf and flower colour and time of flowering: hyssop keeps its medium-green, narrow leaves throughout the winter. Flowers are generally blue-violet produced July–August. There are pink-flowered and white-flowered varieties; also ROCK HYSSOP (*Hyssopus aristatus*) which grows to 30cm (1ft) and makes an ideal edging plant in formal gardens. Flowers are sapphire blue in summer. All hyssop flowers are very attractive to bees and butterflies.

Main usefulness: mainly ornamental. Hyssop makes an attractive low growing hedge ideal for formal herb gardens or to separate beds. The flowering tops and leaves have a bitter, minty taste and can be used to flavour salads and vegetable dishes.

Other virtues: herbalists use an infusion or tea of hyssop in cases of anxiety or mild hysteria. Hyssop also helps expel flatulence and being expectorant, helps relieve bronchial catarrh.

How to keep for later use: cut the flowering tops in August and dry.

LAVENDER

'Then lets meet here, for here are fresh sheets that smell of Lavender, and I am
sure we cannot expect better meat, or better usage in any place.'

Izaak Walton, *Compleat Angler*, 1653

Botanical name: *Lavendula species*   **Family:** *Lamiaceae (Labiatae)*
Type: HP/HHP   **Height:** to 90cm (3ft)
Position preferred: well-drained, sandy limed soils in an open sunny
position. Good drainage is essential. Lavender will not stand having its
roots continually in water. Lavender bushes should be pruned *hard*
immediately after flowering. This produces a sturdy bush less prone to
wind damage and encourages flowering shoots for the following year.
When and how to sow: seed can be sown 6mm (¼in) deep in March–
June. Germination is slow and erratic. Lavender seed is very variable.
Your sowing will probably produce a rather mixed bag of seedlings.
When and how to propagate: it is much better to propagate from stem
cuttings. April/May and August/September are the best times since the
cuttings will be 'softer' and strike more easily than woody cuttings. 5cm
(2in) cuttings are prepared from strongly-growing side shoots and
inserted immediately in a cutting compost. If you find your cuttings
producing flower heads, nip these off as soon as they appear. Lavender
cuttings are slow to take: six to eight weeks in the spring, longer later on.
Cuttings of tender species root more quickly.
Leaf and flower colour and time of flowering: lavender flowers can be
white, pink, blue, purple depending on variety. Leaves can be silver-
grey, grey, grey-green to pale green. Lavender flowers from July to mid-
August. All lavender flowers are attractive to bees and butterflies.
Main usefulness: the current interest in aromatherapy is at last
dispelling the 'old maid' image of lavender. Not before time. Lavender
essential oil is a charming natural flower scent with useful properties.
Lavender oil is widely used in toiletries, perfumes and toilet waters.
Lavender flowers and leaves can be added to fruit salads, summer
punches and wine cups. Lavender jelly is delightfully aromatic. Cooking
with lavender gives a real Provençal flavour to grilled meats and chicken.
Other virtues: an infusion of lavender flowers can be used in cases of
colic and dyspepsia, particularly where these are caused by depression.
Lavender is regarded by herbalists as an anti-depressant hence the
growing use by aromatherapists. Lavender oil has healing and antiseptic
qualities. It is an essential oil that may be used neat on the skin.
Lavender flowers and leaves are considered moth and insect repellants.
How to keep for later use: cut as soon as the first flowers are open. Dry
in bunches hung upside down in a warm, well-ventilated room. Use
dried stems for winter flower arrangements and lavender 'dollies'. Rub off

Mint: *(clockwise)* applemint, eau de cologne mint, spearmint, pineapple mint, peppermint

A field of mustard

flower heads from stems and use in little bags to scent and protect clothes and linen. Save all lavender clippings, spent flower heads – anything! – to use with next summer's barbecue.

Varieties:

DWARF MUNSTEAD produces deep blue flowers of a good fragrance. Leaves are dull grey in summer but look thin and bedraggled in winter. Munstead makes a good low hedge to 45cm (18in) high. Unfortunately, the seed sown as 'Dwarf Munstead' is very variable. Try to get your plants or cuttings from a specialist grower.

FRENCH LAVENDER (*Lavendula stoechas*) is very free flowering with tight whorls of tiny dark purple flowers, the spike topped with purple tufts called bracts. *Lavendula stoechas* is not hardy and needs potting and over-wintering in a greenhouse. French lavender will start to flower as early as March under glass and continue until the autumn. Grow outdoors in summer in a sheltered, well-drained position.

FOLGATE is a dwarf lavender flowering a little earlier than Munstead. Flowers are blue-mauve; leaves grey-green.

GRAPPENHALL makes a large bush to 90cm (3ft). Flowers are bluish-mauve up to 7.5cm (3in) long on spikes to 45cm (18in) produced late July with some flowers later. Leaves are grey-green and keep a good appearance in winter.

HIDCOTE is taller than Munstead and Folgate; grows to 60cm (2ft). Silver-grey leaves are narrow. Flowers are deep rich violet colour ideal for drying on the stem.

Lavendula dentata is a charming, tender lavender from the Mediterranean. The leaves are pale green, toothed rather like ferns; the flowers and bracts pale mauve produced as early as March. The whole plant is warmly aromatic with a balsamic fragrance.

Lavendula stoechas see FRENCH LAVENDER

LODDON PINK has lilac pink flowers which start to show early in July. Bushes grow to 45cm (18in); leaves are grey-green.

SEAL is a tall, erect lavender that looks as if it has been grown to fit the rectangular wood block of a seventeenth century printer. Free flowering, Seal produces in August an abundance of long elegant stems of mid-blue fragrant flowers, somewhere in colour between Grappenhall and Hidcote. Bushes can grow in sheltered conditions to 90cm (3ft) but there is a tendency for branches to split from the plant. Pruning hard, ie cutting the whole plant back to 10cm (4in) above the ground immediately after flowering, will prevent this and encourage more new flowering shoots.

TWICKLE PURPLE grows to 60cm (2ft) producing an abundance of blue-mauve flower heads on 15cm (6in) stems. Leaves are purplish-green. Makes a larger bush than Munstead or Hidcote yet still small enough for a hedge.

WHITE LAVENDER (*Lavendula alba*) is not completely hardy. Outdoors, give it your most sheltered well-drained sunniest spot; or overwinter in pots in a cold greenhouse. Grows to 60cm (2ft). Leaves are grey-green. White fragrant flowers are on 30cm (12in) stems. There is a dwarf form which grows to 20cm (8in).

LEMON BALM

Botanical name: *Melissa officinalis*   **Family:** *Lamiaceae (Labiatae)*
Type: HP   **Height:** 60cm–1m (2–3ft)
Position preferred: sunny position in good deep soil.
When and how to sow: lemon balm seed is very tiny: 1,900 seeds to one gram. Sow April–May in a seed tray. Do not cover the seed but press gently into the compost. Germination is 60 per cent. Seeds will germinate in seven days at 70°F. Transplant seedlings 60cm (2ft) apart.
When and how to propagate: any established plant will give you an abundance of rooted cuttings. Take up a clump from an established plant and break into pieces. Replant the pieces 30cm (1ft) apart. Alternatively, take stem cuttings at any time during the summer.
Leaf and flower colour and time of flowering: nettle shaped, lemon-scented leaves. Small white and pink flowers from mid to late summer. Leaves as well as flowers are very attractive to bees. There is a gold variegated variety.
Main usefulness: use leaves fresh and dried in salad dressings and stuffings. Use dried leaves in pot-pourri.
Other virtues: tea is useful in cases of depression and anxiety.
How to keep for later use: dry young leaves in early summer. Plant can develop mildew later. Leaves will freeze.

LEMON VERBENA

Botanical name: *Aloysia triphylla* syn. *Lippia citriodora*
Family: *Verbenaceae*
Type: HHP   **Height:** up to 3m (10ft) in favourable conditions
Position preferred: full sun and light, well worked soil. Needs abundant water when growing; very little when in store for the winter.
When and how to sow: seed is not obtainable in the UK.
When and how to propagate: cuttings about 90mm (3in) long are taken from the ends of growing shoots. Cuttings can be taken at any time during the summer. Cuttings will root quite quickly and will grow quickly once transplanted. Lemon verbena is usually grown in pots and overwintered in a cold greenhouse. If growing in open ground, plant

Drying herbs in a warm, airy room

Rosemary and rue

38cm (15in) apart. Lift plants in the autumn before the first frosts and store in pots in an unheated greenhouse during the winter. Water pots well before storing, thereafter very sparingly if at all. Plants retain their leaves until the very cold weather, then the leaves die. In March, when you see tiny round green buds re-appearing on the bare stems, spray the stems with water occasionally to encourage sprouting, and start watering and feeding the plants in the pots.

Leaf and flower colour and time of flowering: bright green, long, pointed leaves with a delicious fresh lemon flavour. Tiny lilac flowers are produced in sprays from June–September. New flowering shoots develop below each flowering spray.

Main usefulness: leaves and flowering tops are used to flavour summer drinks and punches. Adds a delicious flavour to fresh fruit salads. Commercially, its essential oil is used in eau de colognes and fresh smelling toilet waters.

Other virtues: lemon verbena taken as a tea is regarded as refreshing and calming. Dry the leaves for use in clothes sachets.

How to keep for later use: pick leaves from fresh growth in the summer and autumn. Lemon verbena dries quickly. Store leaves in a dry, airtight container. Freeze lemon verbena leaves in small packets.

LOVAGE

Botanical name: *Levisticum officinale*   **Family:** *Apiaceae (Umbelliferae)*
Type: HP   **Height:** 1.5–1.8m (5–6ft)

Position preferred: sunny open position in good deep rich soil. Will stand some shade.

When and how to sow: sow seed in July, immediately seeds are ripe. Sow 12mm (½in) deep in drills. Plant out seedlings in the autumn or spring. Lovage dies back completely in winter. It is a good idea to mark your seedlings with a stick so you know where they are due to reappear in the spring. Alternatively, sow in the spring and plant out late summer and autumn. Seeds germinate in eight days at 70°F. Lovage has a long tap root. Transplanting needs to be early.

When and how to propagate: established plants can be lifted in the spring. Replant side shoots. Space 90cm (3ft) apart. Lovage makes a big plant. You only need one plant per family or garden.

Leaf and flower colour and time of flowering: leaves are like large French parsley leaves and smell strongly of celery. Yellow flowers in umbels are produced in July.

Main usefulness: fresh leaves are added to soups, stews and salads to give a celery flavour. Dried leaves and root can be used in winter months. Flavour of lovage is strong so very little is needed.

Other virtues: lovage root as a decoction in water or milk is used in cases of colic, dyspepsia and delayed menstruation. A gargle is beneficial in cases of tonsilitis. Lovage aids digestion and is used in anorexia cases.

How to keep for later use: ripe seed can be collected about mid-August. Dry leaves for winter use. Lift roots from two- to three-year-old plants, wash and dry.

Variety:

SCOTS LOVAGE (*Levisticum scoticum*) is a low growing form. Plant 23cm (9in) apart. Grows to 25cm (10in).

MARIGOLD

'The Marigold that goes to bed wi' th' sun, And with him rises weeping.'

William Shakespeare, *The Winter's Tale*

Botanical name: *Calendula officinalis*   **Family:** *Asteraceae (Compositae)*

Type: HA   **Height:** 60cm (2ft)

Position preferred: any soil, but does best in full sun.

When and how to sow: sow in April under glass; outside in May. Seeds are irregular in shape. Plant 12mm (½in) deep. Plant out or thin to 30cm (1ft) apart. If grown in quantity, try double rows each 30cm (1ft) apart, 60cm (2ft) between each double row.

When and how to propagate: by seed only.

Leaf and flower colour and time of flowering: leaves are a grey green and become mildewed as the nights grow colder. Flowers are round, flat, multi-petalled yellow to orange in colour. As one flower is picked, two more form to take its place. This process is continuous until the frosts. Flowers are at their peak in August.

Main usefulness: marigolds were one of the traditional British pot herbs picked in the summer and dried for winter use in soups and stews. Marigolds were thus a floral bouquet garni that gave a sharp bite to the food and was judged good for the heart and spirits. Marigolds are healing and anti-inflammatory. A useful home hand lotion can be made by infusing fresh marigold flowers in a soothing vegetable oil such as almond. The oil will take on the colour of the flowers.

Other virtues: it is fitting that a herb that takes its name from the Virgin Mary (Mary gold) should have so many virtues. Marigolds are antiseptic, anti-haemorrhagic, styptic. The dried flowers are taken in infusion to treat duodenal and gastric ulcers, and to promote menstruation. Topically, marigolds are used to treat burns, scalds, sebaceous cysts and skin lesions.

How to keep for later use: pick the whole flower heads as soon as the flower heads are fully open and dry. If you hold the flower head in two fingers and turn the wrist sharply, the head will break cleanly from the

Golden sage, tricolour sage, garden sage and red sage

A basket of St John's wort

stem just below the flower. (Marigold flowers open about 9am and close about 3pm, as Shakespeare noticed.) Dry the whole flower head, or pull off the petals and dry these only. The flower petals are quite sticky. Marigold heads freeze well.

Note: French marigolds are not *calendula* but *tagetes*, different family.

MARJORAM

All 'marjorams' and 'oreganos' are of the *Origanum* family. While it is clear that sweet marjoram is a 'marjoram', what is an oregano is much less clear. The dried oregano of the supermarket may be a blend of different plants, some cultivated, some gathered in the Mediterranean wild.

SWEET or KNOTTED MARJORAM
Botanical name: *Origanum majorana* formerly *Marjorana hortensis*
Type: Tender perennial. Treat as HHA   **Height:** 45cm (18in)
Position preferred: well-drained soils in good heart in full sun.
When and how to sow: sow in seed trays early April for planting out mid-May. Transplant to small pots. Space the plants 15cm (6in) apart. Sweet marjoram is intolerant of cold and flower heads may rot in a wet summer. Sweet marjoram responds to feeding. Since sweet marjoram is a perennial, its season can be prolonged until the winter by covering with cloches. Pots of sweet marjoram can be cultivated until the frosts in a cold greenhouse or conservatory.
When and how to propagate: by seed only, although stem cuttings are technically possible.
Leaf and flower colour and time of flowering: grey-green leaves are soft and covered with down. Insignificant creamy flowers in small round heads like knots appear late July to August. The whole plant is fragrantly aromatic.
Main usefulness: sweet marjoram is used fresh or dried to flavour sausages, soups, stews and stuffings; and used fresh in salads. The herb is antioxidant and helps preserve the food with which it is mixed.
Other virtues: leaves can be added to pot-pourri and made into linen sachets for scenting clothes.
How to keep for later use: dry the whole plant when in flower. Rub the dried leaves from the stem.

WILD MARJORAM
Botanical name: *Origanum vulgare*
Type: HP   **Height:** 60cm (2ft)
Position preferred: wild marjoram is a native British herb growing mainly in chalky and lime soils. Wild marjoram likes well-drained and

limed soil in a sunny position but will grow in some shade.

When and how to sow: sow in seed trays pressing the tiny seed into the surface. Transplant to small pots, and subsequently 30cm (1ft) apart.

When and how to propagate: established plants are lifted and rooted offshoots planted 30cm (1ft) apart. Stem cuttings can be taken during the spring and summer.

Flower colour and time of flowering: one of the loveliest herbs in flower with tall stems of dark pink flowers that are as attractive in bud as in full bloom.

Main usefulness: wild marjoram is sharper in flavour than sweet marjoram. It is called oregano in several parts of Europe. Wild marjoram is excellent as a component of bouquet garni; to add to pizzas, meat sauces, soups and stews.

Other virtues: wild marjoram is regarded as good for the stomach, a stimulant and tonic. Wild marjoram is an excellent cut flower. Stems may be dried for winter flower arrangements.

How to keep for later use: dry leaves in July. Dry leaves and flower heads in August.

POT MARJORAM

Botanical name: *Origanum onites*   **Type:** HP   **Height:** 60cm (2ft)
Position preferred: sunny, light, limed soils.
When and how to sow: as wild marjoram.
When and how to propagate: as wild marjoram.
Leaf and flower colour and time of flowering: leaves are lighter in colour and smaller than wild marjoram. Flowers are white or pale pink.
Main usefulness: pot marjoram has a sharper flavour than wild marjoram and can be used for all dishes calling for oregano.
Other virtues: as wild marjoram.
How to keep for later use: as wild marjoram.
Varieties:

GOLDEN MARJORAM and **GOLD TIPPED MARJORAM** are very decorative. Both varieties can be used in the kitchen. Plant at least 60cm (2ft) apart.

WINTER MARJORAM (*O. heracleoticum*) is a short growing marjoram making neat clumps. Close in flavour to pot marjoram.

MARSHMALLOW

Botanical name: *Althaea officinalis*   **Family:** *Malvaceae*
Type: HP   **Height:** 1m (over 3ft)
Position preferred: as its name suggests, marshmallow revels in damp

Soapwort and sorrel

conditions and so enjoys good, fertile soil in a damp position.

When and how to sow: sow 3mm (⅛in) deep in seed trays in the autumn and spring. Transplant seedlings to small pots or final position. If grown commercially, marshmallow is set 40cm (16in) apart in rows 76cm (2ft 6in) apart.

When and how to propagate: offsets can be split from the crown of an established plant and replanted. Stem cuttings will root easily.

Leaf and flower colour and time of flowering: thick fleshy leaves, soft and downy on both sides. Flowers are pale pink 'tending to a blush colour' and appear August–September.

Main usefulness: marshmallow is dumulcent, emollient and healing. Herbalists use the dried, peeled root to treat gastric or duodenal ulcers, and gastritis. The fresh root (peeled) may be used if available. Marshmallow root is also soothing in cases where the mouth and throat are inflamed. Marshmallow leaves are good for bronchitis, respiratory catarrh, and for treating urinary gravel, urethitis and cystitis. A poultice of leaves can be used on wounds and boils.

Other virtues: 'The leaves bruised or rubbed upon any place stung with Bees, Wasps and the like, presently take away the pains, redness and Swellings that rise thereupon.'[1]

How to keep for later use: roots are collected from plants at least two years old, dried and peeled. Leaves are collected when the plant is in flower and dried.

MINT

In flavour terms, there are basically two types of mint: peppermint and spearmint. These two basic flavours are quite distinct but many people find the distinction difficult. Peppermint is sharp, clean, menthol in flavour. Spearmint is warm, aromatic, the traditional flavour of mint sauce. If in doubt, buy a packet of Wrigley's Spearmint chewing gum and a packet of Wrigley's Doublemint chewing gum. For Doublemint, read peppermint. The packets are inexpensive yet Wrigley's use the finest natural oils. Chewing both will be a very good test of your palate as chewing gum has no flavour of its own.

PEPPERMINT

Botanical name: *Mentha piperita*   **Family:** *Lamiaceae (Labiatae)*
Type: HP   **Height:** 90cm (3ft)
Position preferred: mints spread by underground runners. Mints thus grow best in soils rich in organic matter. Mints grow rapidly. What starts off as a small plant with one stem quickly becomes several upright stems

[1]Nicholas Culpeper, *The English Physician*, 1652

which collapse outwardly as the plant develops new runners. Mints need plenty of water when growing.

When and how to sow: peppermint is sterile and does not produce seed. What is offered as 'peppermint' seed may be indeed a mint but not a true peppermint.

When and how to propagate: lift established plants and transplant rooted pieces 10cm (4in) deep in rows 75–90cm (30–36in) wide, plants spaced at 90cm (3ft). Cuttings can be taken from April until the summer and root easily within a few days. Mint cuttings will flop over in the tray shortly after planting. Do not worry. Place overnight in a cool spot, spray gently with water, and the next morning they will be upright.

Leaf and flower colour and time of flowering: leaves are dark green on dark red stems. Peppermint flowers are pale lilac produced in August.

Main usefulness: peppermint is not a culinary herb but one of the finest natural digestives in existence. An infusion of peppermint tea will relieve indigestion and digestive pains, and is helpful with morning sickness. Peppermint tea makes a soothing bed-time drink.

Other virtues: an infusion of peppermint with elderflowers and yarrow is helpful in cases of colds and 'flu.

How to keep for later use: peppermint freezes well. Freeze enough fresh herb for one day's supply of fresh peppermint tea: about 30g fresh herb.

SPEARMINT

Botanical name: *Mentha spicata* formerly *viridis*
Family: *Lamiaceae (Labiatae)*
Type: HP   **Height:** 90cm (3ft)
Position preferred: as peppermint.
When and how to sow: sowing from seed is not advisable.
When and how to propagate: as peppermint.
Leaf and flower colour and time of flowering: aromatic leaves are at their best just before flowering in June and July. Commercial mint growers in the USA wait until 20 per cent of their spearmint is in flower then cut the whole crop. Flowers are small, pinkish-lilac and arranged in whorls. Flowers are very attractive to butterflies.

Main usefulness: spearmint is the 'mint' which is known to every cook and housewife. Chopped leaves of spearmint are added to new potatoes, green peas; put in summer wine cups; made into mint sauce and jelly to eat with lamb. Fresh leaves can be mixed in potato salads, and added to stuffings for poultry and rolled lamb. Spearmint added to mayonnaise for seafood adds a fresh summer taste.

Other virtues: we eat spearmint with lamb as it helps us digest the fatty nature of the meat. Its digestive qualities are similar to peppermint but not so strong. Spearmint's warmer taste is usually preferred by children. Spearmint as a tea is a pleasant home remedy for children's indigestion, sickness and colic.

How to keep for later use: freeze spearmint for winter use. Dry leaves picked in June–July. Make mint vinegars and store fresh leaves in oil.

Varieties:

APPLEMINT (M. *suaveolens*) has round woolly leaves, a spearmint flavour, and a slight apple smell. **BOWLES MINT** (M. *rotundifolia*) is considered a hybrid of the above and M. *spicata*. Applemint and Bowles mint are considered by some to be best for mint sauce. Neither suffer from mint rust but the leaves do mildew in cool weather.

EAU DE COLOGNE MINT (M. *x piperita nm. citrata*) is a splendid mint to grow, for putting in summer wine cups and cordials. Leaves may be dried for pot-pourri. Good in cut flower arrangements since it helps keep away flies.

MULLEIN

Botanical name: *Verbascum thapsus*   **Family:** *Scrophulariaceae*
Type: HB   **Height:** 150cm (5ft)
Position preferred: likes dry, sunny position. Unless given good drainage, mullein will die its first and only winter.
When and how to sow: sow in seed tray March–May. Press the seed into the compost and transplant to small pots when seedlings have second leaves. Put in final position early summer 45cm (18in) apart.
When and how to propagate: by seed only.
Leaf and flower colour and time of flowering: golden yellow flowers in July–August packed tight on tall, stout stems. Leaves are large, silvery grey.
Main usefulness: herbalists use an infusion of dried leaves in cases of bronchitis and 'flu with respiratory catarrh. Mullein is expectorant. Applied externally, 'mullein oil' (the leaves and flowers steeped in olive oil) are regarded as healing when applied to mucous membranes.
Other virtues: the larvae of the mullein or shark moth (*Cucillia verbasci*) are very fond of the plant when in flower. The tall stems which stand the whole winter were tallowed, ie dipped in suet fat and used as a primitive candle. 'It served as a weeke to put into Lamps to burn in former times'.[1]
How to keep for later use: collect the leaves during the flowering period and dry.

MUSTARD

'Sympathy without relief
Is like to Mustard with beef.'

Anon.

[1]William Coles, *Adam in Eden*, 1657

There are three different mustards if classified by the colour of their seeds: BLACK MUSTARD (*Brassica nigra* formerly *Sinapis nigra*), BROWN MUSTARD (*Brassica juncea* formerly *Sinapis juncea*) and WHITE MUSTARD (*Brassica hirta* formerly *Sinapis alba*). Cultivation of all three types is identical.

Botanical name: Brassica species as above   **Family:** *Brassicaceae (Cruciferae)*
Type: HA   **Height:** to 1m (3ft) depending on variety
Position preferred: sandy, loamy soils in dry districts.
When and how to sow: sow 12mm (½in) deep in drills 15cm (6in) apart in March–April.
When and how to propagate: by seed only.
Flower colour and time of flowering: flowers are yellow; large in the case of white mustard. Black mustard has smooth seed pods; white mustard has hairy ones.
Main usefulness: mustard seed is a digestive irritant or stimulant whichever view you take. The seeds are crushed or ground into a flour which is made into table mustard with the addition of wine, vinegar and herbs. White mustard gives flavour; brown and black mustards aroma. The addition of water or other liquids releases the mustard power.
Other virtues: mustard can be eaten as a seedling (mustard and cress) when it is picked eight to ten days after sowing (which can be on the flannel in your bathroom!). When grown outdoors the leaves can be picked as salad greens when more mature. Leaves are peppery in flavour. Mustard flour (ground mustard seed) makes an old-fashioned mustard bath that stimulates the skin and body.
How to keep for later use: pick the seed pods just before the 'fully ripe' stage when the pod will shatter.

NETTLES

'Urtication, or flogging with Nettles, is an old external remedy, which was long practised for chronic rheumatism, and loss of muscular power.'
Dr WT Fernie, *Herbal Simples*, 1914.

Botanical name: *Urtica diorica*   **Family:** *Urticaceae*
Type: HP   **Height:** 150cm (5ft)
Position preferred: moist, open, rich soils. Will tolerate some shade.
When and how to sow: seed unobtainable but can be collected in the wild. Seed falls as it ripens so is difficult to gather.
When and how to propagate: lift an established clump virtually anytime and transplant rooted pieces. Cut off any tall tops before replanting.
Leaf and flower colour and time of flowering: leaves are heart-shaped, toothed and pointed, light green in the spring, darker later. Whole plant

is downy and covered with stinging hairs. Flowers are green, produced in clusters from June to September. Rubbing with a dock leaf gives relief from the stings.

Main usefulness: nettle was a traditional spring pot-herb that was cooked like spinach, served as spring greens or in soup. Nettle contains ascorbic acid (natural Vitamin C). Nettle tea was drunk in the spring to cleanse the blood. Herb beers were made in the spring from nettles, dandelion and clivers, to be drunk in the summer and at harvest-time.

Other virtues: dried nettles in infusion are used by herbalists to treat nervous eczema. Nettles are anti-haemorrhagic, used to treat nose and other internal bleeding.

How to keep for later use: the whole plant should be gathered in May and June before the herb flowers. If gathered later, the leaves contain gritty crystals. Drying is best done in bunches of six to eight stems tied in a bundle and hung where warm air can freely circulate between the stems. Any discoloured or insect-eaten leaves should be removed. When dry, cut and store in airtight containers. Nettles can be frozen but not unfrozen. To use as a tea, pour boiling water on the nettles without thawing them.

OREGANO *see Marjoram*

PARSLEY

Botanical name: *Petroselinum crispum*   **Family:** *Apiaceae (Umbelliferae)*
Type: HB   **Height:** 30–45cm (1–1½ft)

Position preferred: moist, rich soil with some shade. Parsley grows well only when its roots are cool. For this reason, plants should be in shade for part of the day. Watering in the summer is beneficial.

When and how to sow: parsley seed is slow and erratic in germination, particularly in early spring when soil conditions can be cold. Soaking the seeds in water for twenty-four hours before sowing helps germination. Sowing seed in compartmentalised trays and transplanting to open ground when weather improves gives better results. Sow seeds no deeper than ¼in. Parsley should be planted in single rows 45–56cm (18–22in) apart or double rows 90cm (3ft) apart. Space plants 10–20cm (4–8in) apart. Sow and plant in autumn for winter supplies.

When and how to propagate: only from seed.

Leaf and flower colour and time of flowering: dark green, curled, crisp leaves. Flowers produced in the second year are greenish-yellow, produced in flat sprays. Parsley dies after producing seed.

Main usefulness: parsley is the best known and most used culinary herb. Fresh leaves are used to garnish meat, poultry and vegetable dishes. Parsley should always be used with garlic.

Other virtues: parsley is a rich source of Vitamin C. It is a diuretic and helpful in cases of painful menstruation. Parsley oil has been shown to stimulate regeneration of the liver. Parsley is anti-rheumatic and antimicrobial.

How to keep for later use: dried parsley has very little taste. Parsley freezes very well. Frozen parsley keeps its flavour. This is the recommended way to keep.

Varieties:

FRENCH/ITALIAN PARSLEY (*Petroselinum* var. *neapolitanum*) is similar in taste and characteristics to var. *crispum* but has flat, non-crisped leaves.

HAMBURG PARSLEY (*Petroselinum tuberosum*) is grown mainly for its large edible roots.

PENNYROYAL

'There is hardly a Country Lasse of sixteen years old but knows that Pennyroyal boyled in Beer and drunk, provoketh the courses.'

William Coles, *Adam in Eden*, 1657.

Botanical name: *Mentha pulegium*　　**Family:** *Lamiaceae (Labiatae)*
Type: HP　　**Height:** 30cm (1ft)
Position preferred: damp, fertile soils with some shade.
When and how to sow: sow March–May. Press the seed into the compost of a seed tray and keep moist.
When and how to propagate: stem cuttings will root readily. Cut stems below the lower leaf nodes. Take root cuttings by lifting established plants and breaking into small pieces. Plant 2ft apart when in a border.
Leaf and flower colour and time of flowering: pennyroyal has small, bright green oval leaves with a rather sharp acrid peppermint smell. Numerous small mauve flowers are produced in clusters on short stems above the spreading plant in August–September.
Main usefulness: ornamental spreading plant that will carpet a shady corner or make a 'lawn' smelling deliciously of peppermint. Useful also for making a scented seat. When planting a pennyroyal lawn or seat, plant 6–8in apart.
Other virtues: pennyroyal in infusion is used to relieve colds, treat colic and promote menstruation. **Its use is inadvisable in pregnancy since pennyroyal can induce miscarriage.**
How to keep for later use: dry the leaves and flowers in summer.

ROSEMARY

Botanical name: *Rosmarinus officinalis*　　**Family:** *Lamiaceae (Labiatae)*
Type: HP　　**Height:** 1m (3ft 4in), higher against walls.

Position preferred: well-drained sandy soils in full sun. Rosemary does best in a sheltered spot, especially as it grows taller. If heavy snow is threatened, tie the branches in a loose bundle since they break easily. Rosemary grows well against a wall.

When and how to sow: seed sown in April–May in seed trays will produce good-sized plants by the autumn. Seed is very variable. Sow 12mm (½in) deep and transplant to small pots. Plant at least 90cm (3ft) apart. Once rosemary is at its maximum height, it will grow sideways.

When and how to propagate: cuttings 7.5–10cm (3–4in) in length root in about fourteen days given bottom heat of 75°F. Cuttings should be 'soft', ie not woody, taken from the top of the branches or strong side shoots. Cuttings can be taken from March to September, and can be overwintered as rooted cuttings in a greenhouse for potting in the spring. Pinch out the tops of the cuttings when transplanting, this encourages the plant to branch and grow bushy.

Leaf and flower colour and time of flowering: leaves are thin, narrow, dark green, lighter underneath. Flowers are numerous, small, pale blue, tucked in tightly to the main stem. Rosemary will start to flower in February in a mild winter and continue until May. Useful bee plant when few other plants are flowering.

Main usefulness: a wonderful culinary herb to use with roast lamb, pork chops, steaks, in stews, soups, sausages and stuffings. Its culinary use is well-founded since rosemary has antioxidant as well as carminative properties. Rosemary essential oil is an ingredient in eau-de-colognes, shampoos and hair tonics. A few drops of rosemary essential oil in the rinsing water will leave the hair shiny and pleasantly fragrant.

Other virtues: rosemary tea is useful in cases of tension, tense nervous headaches and depression. Rosemary oil is used in embrocations and rubbing oils to stimulate the skin.

How to keep for later use: leaves can be frozen or dried but since rosemary is evergreen, it is always available for use in your garden. Woody pieces or prunings should be kept for summer barbecues.

Varieties:

MISS JESSUP'S UPRIGHT is hardy; its leaves lighter in colour and flowers a paler blue.

Varieties such as **PINK ROSEMARY, WHITE ROSEMARY, UPRIGHT BLUE** and many other varieties which one suspects have been brought back by enthusiasts from Mediterranean holidays are not fully hardy. Grown in tubs they can usually be overwintered in a cold greenhouse.

PROSTRATE ROSEMARY and other trailing varieties are tender and need heat in winter to survive.

Tansy, southernwood and sweet cicely

Violets and woodruff

John Parkinson in *Paradisi in Sole* (1629) talks of a **Gilded Rosemary**, the leaves striped or edged with a 'faire gold yellow colour'. This rare gold-variegated rosemary can still be found growing at Hatfield House in the famous herb garden.

RUE

Botanical name: *Ruta graveolens*   **Family:** *Rutaceae*
Type: HP   **Height:** 90cm (3ft)
Position preferred: well-drained ordinary soil in sunny position.
When and how to sow: sow seed in April in trays, pressing the seed into the compost.
When and how to propagate: take stem cuttings in late spring and summer.
Leaf and flower colour and time of flowering: leaves are blue-green and finely cut. Flowers are soft yellow with four petals and a green centre. **Jackman's Rue** has much bluer leaves. There is also a pretty variegated version whose leaves are green and gold. The plant is heavily aromatic with a very distinctive strong smell.
Main usefulness: an infusion of rue is used by herbalists in cases of suppressed menstruation. Rue is also antitussive, ie helps stop coughing.
Other virtues: rue was regarded as an antipestilential herb. Bunches were hung to rid the house of flies. Judges carried sprigs to help ward off gaol fever.
How to keep for later use: the plant is evergreen although the leaves are not so noticeable in winter.

SAFFRON

'The English are rendered sprightly by a liberal use of saffron in sweetmeats and broth.'

Lord Bacon, *History of Life and Death.*

Botanical name: *Crocus sativus*   **Family:** *Iridaceae*
Type: HP bulb   **Height:** 7.5cm (4in)
Position preferred: rich, light well drained soils in full sun.
When and how to sow: saffron comes from the flowers of an autumn-flowering crocus. Sow the corms in August and September 7.5cm (3in) deep, 5cm (2in) apart. Lift the corms in June and July when the foliage has turned yellow; dry and store in a cool place until re-planting.
When and how to propagate: as above. Lifted corms will produce small new corms which can be grown on to a larger, flowering size.
Leaf and flower colour and time of flowering: violet-blue flowers are produced before the leaves in September and October. There is only one flower per plant. Six to nine narrow leaves are produced.
Main usefulness: saffron is the most expensive spice in the world. Until

recently, weight for weight, saffron was the same price as gold. Fortunately, you need very little to add colour and fragrance to rice and fish dishes, saffron flour and buns. Too much is overpowering. A good guide is that one stigma will flavour a dish for six people. The flavour of saffron is warm, subtle, rather earthy; the colour a strong yellow. It is essential in 'paella', a traditional Spanish rice dish of fish and/or chicken. Saffron is also an ingredient in traditional English barley sugar. In cooking, either steep the strands in hot water for ten minutes; add strands to hot oil; or dry roast at 300°F for one to two minutes.

Other virtues: saffron is used in Indian and Chinese medicine as a stimulant and in melancholia. Saffron is known to be quite toxic and should never be taken in large amounts.

How to keep for later use: the flowers are picked, peeled and the three deep red stigmas plucked out. The stigmas are then dried. It takes 75,000 flowers to produce 225,000 stigmas which when dried will be 454g (1lb) of dried saffron strands. You can see why saffron is expensive, especially as it is only possible to harvest the stigmas by hand.

Saffron substitutes: because of saffron's high cost, substitution is common. **Turmeric** (*Curcuma longa*), a yellow aromatic, pungent root of East Indian origin is most often used particularly in Indian and West Indian cooking. **Marigold** (*Calendula officinalis*) petals will also add colour and a sharp flavour. **Safflower** (*Carthamus tinctorius*), sometimes called Mexican saffron, is used to adulterate saffron.

SAGE

Botanical name: *Salvia officinalis*   **Family:** *Lamiaceae (Labiatae)*
Type: HP   **Height:** 60cm (2ft)
Position preferred: sunny, well-drained light soil. Sage bushes deteriorate after a few years and will need replacing with fresh plants. Fresh plants should be planted in a different place. Like roses, sage does not do well if replanted in the same soil.

When and how to sow: seed started in March indoors or sown outdoors in April/May will produce strong plants by the autumn. Seeds are sown 12mm (½in) deep in drills or seed trays. Germination at 70°F is nine days. Final planting distance is 45cm (18in).

When and how to propagate: sage can be propagated by cuttings or layering. Layering is where side shoots are pinned to the ground and covered with soil. These will root in about eight weeks. Alternatively, soil is earthed up round an established plant so that all the side shoots have their lower parts buried in soil. The plant is later lifted and divided when the side shoots have rooted. This takes eight weeks. Cuttings can be taken from March to September and root quickly with bottom heat.

Leaf and flower colour and time of flowering: leaves are soft to the touch, about 5cm (2in) long and oval in shape. Garden sage leaves are grey-green in colour. Small, purple flowers cover the flowering stems in July–August. Flowers are very attractive to bees.

Main usefulness: most people know of sage through its association with sage and onion stuffing, traditionally used with pork and goose. Sage's warmly aromatic taste adds flavour, particularly to white meat and poultry. Its inclusion in stuffings and sausages helps the body cope with the fattiness and hence indigestability of the meat. Sage is astringent and has carminative properties. The flavour is strong, so use sparingly.

Other virtues: sage is a useful antiseptic. 'Gargles likewise are made with Sage ... with some Honey put thereto, to wash sore Mouths and throats', advice from Nicholas Culpeper some 300 years ago and still excellent today. An infusion of sage is useful in cases of flatulent dyspepsia. Sage tea or infusion used to be drunk in May in the belief that it would encourage long life.

How to keep for later use: leaves can be dried or frozen. Make sage vinegar during the summer. Make sage butter and freeze.

Varieties:

GOLDEN SAGE (*Salvia officinalis* var. *Icterina*) has variegated gold-green leaves and pale purple flowers, stems of which are infrequent.

RED SAGE (*Salvia officinalis* var. *purpurascens*) flowers more readily. The colour of the flowers is similar to ordinary sage and contrasts cheerfully with the dark purple leaves.

BROAD LEAVED SAGE has larger more downy leaves and does not flower. Flavour is milder than ordinary sage.

TRICOLOUR SAGE (*Salvia officinalis* var. *tricolor*) has very pretty narrow leaves of red, cream and green but is not at all hardy. It is best to lift plants in the autumn, overwinter in a cool greenhouse and re-plant in the spring.

CLARY SAGE (*Salvia sclarea*) is a tall striking plant with pale purple and white flowers and purple bracts to 120cm (4ft). Clary sage is usually grown as a biennial. The essential oil is used as a fixative in the perfume industry. Clary sage has the reputation of clearing the sight. Its seeds when soaked are very mucilaginous and were used to draw grit from the eye and splinters from the skin.

PINEAPPLE SAGE (*Salvia elegans* formerly *Salvia rutilans*) is a tender perennial with leaves that smell of pineapple, and scarlet flowers.

ST JOHN'S WORT

Botanical name: *Hypericum perforatum*   **Family:** *Hypericaceae*
Type: HP   **Height:** 90cm (3ft)

Position preferred: sheltered sunny position in ordinary soil.

When and how to sow: sow in seed boxes pressing seed into the surface of the compost.

When and how to propagate: stem cuttings can be taken in the spring before flowering.

Leaf and flower colour and time of flowering: pale green leaves and bright yellow five petalled flowers from June to August. Seeds are small, round and black.

Main usefulness: St John's Wort as *Hypericum* is extensively used in homeopathic medicine for the treatment of wounds and injured nerves. St John's Wort is sedative and has been used in cases of children's bed-wetting.

Other virtues: St John's Wort is used with witch hazel to treat haemorrhoids and bruising; and with marigold as a mouthwash and to treat bruising.

How to keep for later use: cut and dry the flowers and plant tops during or just before the flowering period. Infuse the flowers and herb in vegetable oil and use for rubbing parts affected with sciatica and neuralgia.

SALAD BURNET

'The greatest use is to put a few leaves into a cup with Claret wine ... accounted a helpe to make the heart merrie.'

John Parkinson, *Paradisi in Sole*, 1629.

Botanical name: *Poterium sanguisorba*   **Family:** *Rosaceae*

Type: HP   **Height:** 45cm (18in)

Position preferred: open, sunny position in ordinary soil.

When and how to sow: sow in April in seed trays or outside. Transplant to 30cm (1ft) apart.

When and how to propagate: roots can be divided in the autumn.

Leaf and flower colour and time of flowering: salad burnet forms a dense rosette of leaves from which stems of small green regularly cut leaves spray out like two little wings. The flowers are rose red and small, '... borne in on an inflorescence somewhat like a green pinecone,'[1] and appear in July. The flower heads should be removed if being grown for leaves. When the leaves become coarse, cut the whole plant back. New leaves will soon spring forth.

Main usefulness: salad burnet is a cooling herb whose leaves smell and taste of cucumber. It can be used in spring salads and to add to summer wine cups to which 'it yeeldeth a certaine grace in the drinking'.[2]

[1]Helen Morgenthau Fox, *Gardening with Herbs*, New York 1933
[2]John Gerarde, *The Herball*, 1633

Other virtues: its latin name *sanguisorba* suggests that it is a styptic, an infusion being used as an astringent.

How to keep for later use: salad burnet is virtually evergreen. A little protection in the winter will ensure a regular supply of leaves if needed although this is really a herb for spring and summer use.

SANTOLINA

'But there is an use, wherein this exceeds that of Southernwood, and that is to make Knots, Trailes, and other Compartiments in the Gardens of Noble Personages.'

William Coles, *Adam in Eden*, 1657.

The family name of a group of shrubby aromatic herbs commonly called 'cotton lavender', sometimes 'French lavender'.

Botanical name: *Santolina chamaecyparissus*
Family: *Asteraceae (Compositae)*
Type: HP   **Height:** 90cm (3ft)
Position preferred: light, well-drained soils in full sun.
When and how to sow: not usually grown from seed.
When and how to propagate: cuttings are taken from April onwards when new growth will be well underway. Cuttings root readily. Plants should be spaced about 90cm (3ft) apart since growth is generous. Mature plants sprawl. Regular clipping helps preserve shape. Start in April when new growth begins.
Leaf and flower colour and time of flowering: leaves are silver grey and aromatic. Flowers are golden yellow, disc-shaped and appear in July–August.
Main usefulness: santolina can be planted as a low hedge and clipped to make parterres, knot and formal herb gardens.
Other virtues: santolina is often included in dried herb moth mixtures.
How to keep for later use: not used in cooking nor medically. Dry for moth mixtures.

SAVORY

A strangely neglected herb since its aromatic taste combines a touch of thyme, a hint of marjoram, a little rosemary. It should be as universally used as parsley. The French are wiser and use their *sariette* as a salt substitute. There is an annual and several perennial forms. All are very attractive to bees and butterflies when in flower. **Family:** *Lamiacae (Labiatae)*

SUMMER SAVORY
Botanical name: *Satureja hortensis*
Type: HA   **Height:** 50cm (20in)

Position preferred: given full sun, summer savory will grow in any soil type.

When and how to sow: outside in April in drills 6mm (¼in) deep. Thin to 23cm (9in). Sow in March in seed trays and transplant. If transplanting from seed trays to the garden, summer savory is one to grow in compartmentalised trays. Seed is true to type with little variation. Seedlings respond to feeding.

When and how to propagate: by seed only in April. Seedlings should be planted or thinned to 15cm (6in) apart in rows 30cm (1ft) apart.

Leaf and flower colour and time of flowering: leaves are small and pointed like thyme leaves. Summer savory is not really a very attractive plant in the herb garden, thin and sparse with tiny heliotrope flowers in August. The bees however appreciate it greatly.

Main usefulness: traditionally, savory is used to flavour broad beans, lentils and other dried vegetables. Savory is excellent with all meats, with poultry, in sausages and stuffings. Summer savory is more sweetly aromatic than winter savory.

Other virtues: summer savory is regarded as a stimulant, good for the stomach and is carminative.

How to keep for later use: hang the herb in bunches when in full flower to dry.

WINTER SAVORY

Botanical name: *Satureja montana*
Type: HP   **Height:** 37cm (15in)
Position preferred: well-drained, light, sandy soils in full sun.

When and how to sow: seed can be sown in April in seed trays. Seed available commercially is very variable. You will get erect plants, lazy lax plants and even creeping ones. Some of these will die back completely in the winter. Others will keep their leaves as they should to justify their name.

When and how to propagate: by cuttings late spring, summer and early autumn. Choose a plant that you know keeps its winter leaves.

Leaf and flower colour and time of flowering: leaves are thin, dark green, similar to hyssop and very aromatic. Flowers are almost white, pale purple and pink. Winter savory flowers late August–September and is a valuable late source of pollen.

Main usefulness: as summer savory. Winter savory is sharper in flavour, excellent in stews and stuffings. Add to oil and vinegar dressings.

Other virtues: as summer savory.

How to keep for later use: cut and freeze young green branches and leaves. Pick leaves and dry.

Other perennial varieties:
CREEPING SAVORY (*Satureja repanda*) is a creeping version with white flowers that contrast attractively with the brighter green foliage. Flowers appear early August and continue to September.
S. coerula is a late flowering variety with intense blue flowers. It is a small plant suitable for the rock garden.

SOAPWORT

'It is of a somewhat an ungrateful taste, and therefore it must be reserved for the poorer sort.'

John Gerarde, *The Herball*, 1633

Botanical name: *Saponaria officinalis*   **Family:** *Caryophyllaceae*
Other common names: Bouncing Bet, Bruisewort
Type: HP   **Height:** 90cm (3ft)
Position preferred: open sunny position with plenty of room for its creeping roots to spread. Soapwort can be invasive.
When and how to sow: sow broadcast in open ground in its final position; or in 12mm (½in) drills in seed trays transplanting to small pots when large enough to handle.
When and how to propagate: stem cuttings will root in eight days at 70°F.
Flower colour and time of flowering: soapwort produces tall stems of fragrant pale pink flowers which are at their best mid-August. Good plant for an herbaceous border.
Main usefulness: Lady Meade-Featherstonhaugh, president of Culpeper and the Herb Society in the 1960's pioneered the revival of soapwort as a safe cleanser of delicate, historic fabrics. Examples of her work can be seen at Uppark where she lived, Sion Park where she restored the wall hangings in the Long Gallery, Bowhill and Williamsburg, Virginia where she advised on the cleaning of George Washington's coat. A decoction of soapwort leaves and roots was brushed on fabrics and when dry, brushed off. When asked where the dirt had gone, her inevitable reply was that the herb had eaten it. Wall hangings were spread overnight on the lawn to attract the dew and then immersed in baths of saponaria solution.
Other virtues: an infusion of saponaria leaves can be used as a gentle shampoo. Formerly, an infusion was also used to bathe bruises, and taken internally for scrofulous conditions. Due to its saponin content, the latter is not recommended today.
How to keep for later use: pick the leaves during the summer and dry. Lift the roots in the autumn, wash and dry.

SORREL

In the making of salads 'imparting so grateful a quickness to the rest as supplies the want of Orange, and lemon; and, therefore never to be excluded.'

John Evelyn, *Acetaria*, 1699.

Botanical name: *Rumex acetosa*   **Family:** *Polygonaceae*

Type: HP   **Height:** 60cm (2ft)

Position preferred: rich, open, moist soils with plenty of humus.

When and how to sow: sow 12mm (1in) deep in rows 45cm (18in) apart in March. Thin the seedlings to 30cm (1ft) apart in the row.

When and how to propagate: divide the roots in March. Replant 30cm (1ft) apart. Water well after replanting.

Leaf and flower colour and time of flowering: large fleshy green leaves from April onwards. Red spikes of red, green and orange flowers turning crimson. If you are growing for leaves, you cut off the flowering stems as soon as you see them.

Tarragon and valerian

Main usefulness: sorrel leaves are acidic and make an excellent green sauce for fatty meats like lamb. Sorrel is an essential ingredient for the classic *Soupe a la Bonne Femme* which Auguste Kettner, the celebrated Victorian restauranteur, claimed symbolised womanhood: the acidity of sorrel and the softness of cream. 'There is a gracious sauvity in the soup, with a subacid flavour to remind one pleasantly of the little gleams of temper'.[1] Mrs Leyel recommended that sorrel should be cooked like spinach but mixed with a little lettuce to make it less bitter.[2] Use sorrel in omelettes and soups.

Other virtues: sorrel is of the dock family which is known to be cleansing in its action.

How to keep for later use: freeze leaves in the quantities you will require for soups, omelettes and sauces.

Variety: Sorrel is sometimes called French Sorrel but this is more correctly applied to **Rumex scutatus** which is less acidic. *R. scutatus* has smaller, pale yellowish-green leaves. Plants are set at 15cm (6in) intervals in rows 30cm (1ft) apart. Watering is recommended in hot weather.

SOUTHERNWOOD

'It is said that if a branch of Southernwood be laid under one's Bed, Pillow or Bolster, it provoketh carnal copulation, and resisteth all enchantments that hinder the same'.

William Coles, *Adam in Eden, 1657.*

Botanical name: *Artemisia abrotanum*   **Family:** *Asteraceae (Compositae)*
Type: HP   **Height:** to 1.2m (4ft)
Position preferred: full sun in ordinary soil.
When and how to sow: seed not available.
When and how to propagate: by cuttings, late spring/early summer.
Leaf colour: grey-green aromatic leaves produced on erect branches. In winter, the leaves die leaving the branches with spent remains of leaves until a promising little tuft of fresh green leaves appears on the top of each branch in spring.
Main usefulness: ornamental. The finely cut, soft, grey-green foliage gives a lovely soft background.
Other virtues: herbalists use an infusion of southernwood in cases of delayed menstruation; and to treat thread worms in children. Leaves are dried and used in sachets to deter moths.
How to keep for later use: the leaves and tops are collected June–August and dried.

[1]*Kettner's Book of the Table*, ES Dallas, 1877
[2]*The Gentle Art of Cookery*, Mrs CF Leyel and Miss Olga Hartley, London, 1925

SUCCORY *see Chicory*
SWEET BASIL *see Basil*
SWEET BAY *see Bay*
SWEET CICELY

'So fine and pleasant in Sallets as no other is comparable to it, and give a better relish to any other herbe is put with it.'

John Parkinson, *Theathrum Botanicum*, 1640.

Botanical name: *Myrrhis odorata*   **Family:** *Apiaceae (Umbelliferae)*
Type: HP   **Height:** 60cm (2ft)
Position preferred: dampish position with some shade.
When and how to sow: sweet cicely seed needs a period of cold if it is to germinate. Sow 5cm (2in) deep in seed trays in the autumn and expose the seeds to the winter's elements. If sowing in the spring and the weather is mild, put the seed tray in a fridge where the temperature should be just above freezing and leave for about fourteen days.
When and how to propagate: divide the roots in early spring and re-plant 30cm (1ft) apart.
Leaf and flower colour and time of flowering: fresh, bright green, soft lacy leaves appear in spring followed by stalks of white flowers in May–June. These are succeeded by tight clusters of black, shiny seeds.
Main usefulness: a natural sweetener useful for diabetic or slimming diets. Stew the leaves with rhubarb and gooseberries.
Other virtues: fresh leaves which have an anise flavour may be chopped and added to spring salads when they add a 'marvellous good relish to all the rest'. Roots were once boiled as a vegetable, and candied like angelica 'to preserve the spirits from infection at the time of the Plague'.
How to keep for later use: seed is ripe by first week in July.

TANSY

'Want of eating this Herb in Spring make people sickly in summer.'

Nicholas Culpeper, *English Physician*, 1652.

Botanical name: *Tanacetum vulgare*   **Family:** *Asteraceae (Compositae)*
Type: HP   **Height:** 150cm (5ft)
Position preferred: sunny open position in any soil. Tansy is quite hard work in the garden! It is very invasive so give it plenty of room and contain it once a year by chopping round the clump, pulling out roots which are going too far.
When and how to sow: sow in spring or autumn 1.5cm (½in) deep. If flower heads are left to seed, you will find tansy seedlings everywhere.

When and how to propagate: lift in autumn and spring and replant rooted pieces. Plant at least 120cm (4ft) apart.

Leaf and flower colour and time of flowering: dark green, feathery, very aromatic leaves. Flat heads of yellow button flowers appear June–October. There is a variety **Tanacetum vulgare** var. **crispum** whose leaves are curled like parsley.

Main usefulness: a decoction of tansy is used by herbalists topically to treat scabies. Tansy is a powerful worm killer and is given as an infusion. **Tansy should not be used in pregnancy.**

Other virtues: in the seventeenth century, fresh young leaves of tansy were fried with eggs in the spring to clean the stomach after the winter and the salt fish of Lent. Tansy cakes were made for the Easter festival.

How to keep for later use: flower heads can be dried for winter arrangements. Dried leaves are used in moth mixtures.

TARRAGON

'The name is said to be equivalent to Dragon – the tortuous form of its roots suggesting the dragon's tail. It is a dragon much esteemed, and wagging its tail most agreeably in a green Mayonnaise, in a Bearnaise sauce, in a dish of chicken a l'estragon, and in a ravigote which brightens many a salad.'

ES Dallas, *Kettner's Book of Table*, 1877.

Botanical name: *Artemisia dracunculus*   **Family:** *Asteracea (Compositae)*
Other name: French tarragon
Type: HP in warm districts   **Height:** 60–90cm (2–3ft)
Position preferred: warm, sunny, light soil. Plant 30cm (1ft) apart in rows 45cm (18in) apart. Tarragon needs winter protection in cold areas. Cover the beds with loosely shaken straw in the late autumn. Remove in March when you see the new bright green shoots appearing.

When and how to sow: does not grow from seed.

When and how to propagate: *root* cuttings can be taken from established clumps in the spring. Pieces of root about 90mm (3in) long are re-planted. *Stem* cuttings are taken from healthy main shoots and should be 2in long when prepared. The leaves should be stripped from the bottom 1in of stem. Cuttings need planting in a compartmentalised tray where each hole in the tray has an open bottom. Fill the holes in the tray with Perlite. Insert the cuttings to the depth of the hole and firm Perlite round the cutting. Water the tray and leave in a cool place overnight. In the morning, place the tray filled with cuttings on bottom heat of 75°–80°F. This bottom heat should provide enough heat to dry out the plugs overnight to just moist. Water enough to repeat the process daily. Temperature at night should not drop below 60°F. The cuttings should root in about nine to twelve days. When you can see the roots coming through the bottom of the holes, feed the cuttings every three days. Remove the cuttings from heat about a week after rooting and continue to feed. The rooting process will be slower when there are shorter days and cloudy weather.

Leaf and flower colour and time of flowering: leaves are about 5cm (2in) long, thin, bright green and very aromatic. Flowers are hardly noticeable and do not ripen seed.

Main usefulness: essential part of all French cooking. Tarragon gives Bearnaise sauce its special taste and is delicious with chicken and fish.

Other virtues: French tarragon has been reported to be antioxidant and antifungal. Tarragon is regarded as good for the stomach.

How to keep for later use: cut stems in the summer and strip off the leaves. The leaves should be a bright green colour. Throw away leaves that are eaten or yellow. Store the leaves in oil (*see* basil); dry in a warm place then store in airtight containers; freeze small quantities. Tarragon freezes very well. Freezing is the preferred method.

Note: there is another tarragon, **Russian tarragon** (*Artemisia dracunculoides*), which is sometimes offered as tarragon either as plants or seeds. Although more hardy than French tarragon, Russian tarragon is far inferior in taste and not worth growing.

THYME

'If it were not so common as at tables, it would be more regarded as a medicine.'
John Hill, *The British Herbal,* 1756

Botanical name: *Thymus vulgaris*   **Family:** *Lamiaceae (Labiatae)*
Type: HP   **Height:** 20cm (8in)

Position preferred: full sun in light, well-drained gravelly soil.

When and how to sow: sow in March–May, pressing the tiny seed into the surface of the compost. Thyme seed is very variable. Transplant seedlings 30–45cm (1–1½ft) apart.

When and how to propagate: by cuttings about 2.5cm (1in) long inserted two or three together. When transplanted, the cutting should be topped to encourage bushiness of growth.

Flower colour and time of flowering: flowers are over by endJune. The flowers of all varieties of thyme are very attractive to bees and butterflies.

Main usefulness: thyme is pungent and full of flavour, especially good with meats, roast lamb, pork, stews and grilled fish.

Other virtues: an important medical herb. Its anti-tussive and expectorant qualities are helpful in cases of bronchitis. It is bactericidal and antiseptic. Gargling with an infusion of thyme is good for sore throats.

How to keep for later use: save some sprigs in olive oil. Cut and dry whole branches. Put under chops when grilling. Dry, rub off the leaves and store.

Varieties:

BROAD-LEAVED THYME (*Thymus pulegioides*) is at its best in mid-July/early August when it produces strong, upright mauve-pink flowers in profusion. Planted 30cm (1ft) apart, it makes a pleasing low hedge.

CARAWAY THYME (*Thymus herba barona*) is a creeping dark leaved thyme that makes a dense mat. Flowers are rose-purple in June. Leaves were used to flavour baron of beef.

DIDI (*Thymus mastichina* x unknown), a very fragrant creeping thyme, free flowering, strong growth.

DOONE VALLEY is a spreading variegated thyme that forms a dense carpet with purple flowers in mid-July.

GOLD VARIEGATED THYME is a taller thyme, very decorative with pink flowers late June.

GOLDEN THYME (*Thymus vulgaris aureus*) grows to 15cm (6in) high and spreads.

LEMON THYME (*Thymus citriodorus*) is a wonderful blend of sharp lemon and warm thyme. Erect growing, it needs cutting back to produce sprigs for cooking.

PORLOCK is one of the earliest thymes in flower. The erect spreading foliage is greyish, the flowers pink.

SILVER POSIE (*Thymus vulgaris*) flowers in late June/early July. It is erect growing, about 21cm (9in) high, its pale mauve flowers contrasting beautifully with the silver-grey foliage.

SILVER QUEEN (*Thymus citriodorus*) is similar in appearance to Silver Posie but slightly smaller and less hardy. Its leaves are lemon scented.

THYMUS AZORICUS, a bouncy low growing thyme with little volcanic clumps of pale-purple flowers late June, the green foliage spreading like lava across the ground.

THYMUS MASTICHINA leaves have a strong eucalyptus or camphoraceous smell. Tiny white flowers are produced in 'white downie heads' in August. This is the Herb Masticke of the old herbals. *Thymus mastichina* is not hardy and should be overwintered in a cold greenhouse and 'there maintained with great care and diligence from the injury of our cold climate'.

THYMUS ODORATISSIMUS has large pale mauve flowers which are covered in bees late June/early July. The leaves are long, green-grey with rather straggly prostrate stems.

WHITE THYME (*Thymus albus*) is a bright green creeping thyme with tiny stems and leaves. Produces small white flowers late June/early July.

WILD or CREEPING THYME (*Thymus serpyllum*) is a native British plant also listed in the *British Herbal Pharmacopaeia*. Wild thyme can be used in cooking as all other thymes. Medicinally, it is used by herbalists to treat bronchitis, whooping cough and laryngitis. Wild thyme is antiseptic, antimicrobial and healing in its action. The flowering branches rise from the creeping stems. Wild thyme flowers in late June/early July. Flowers are lilac.

VALERIAN

Botanical name: *Valeriana officinalis*   **Family:** *Valerianaceae*
Type: HP   **Height:** 120cm (4ft)
Position preferred: moist, rich well-drained soil. Some shade is fine since valerian likes cool conditions.
When and how to sow: sow seeds in autumn after ripening. Roots will be ready for harvesting at the end of the second season after sowing.
When and how to propagate: divide roots in spring and autumn. Replant offsets 30cm (1ft) apart. Small offsets may need two years to produce roots big enough to harvest. Large offsets will produce good roots in one year.
Flower colour and time of flowering: flowers are small, pale, flesh in colour in tight clusters on stems above the leaves. Valerian flowers from June until September. Flowers should be removed to encourage production of the root.
Main usefulness: valerian is a natural tranquiliser, an infusion or decoction of the dried roots being taken in cases of hysteria, tension and excitability. Recent research has shown valerian improves sleep quality without the hangover effect of barbiturates. Valerian is also helpful in cases of colic and cramp.
Other virtues: the fresh and dried roots have a strong aromatic smell. If you cat is not a catnep freak, he is likely to be a valerian one! Cats roll in valerian as in catnep; and similarly a cat will enjoy playing with a valerian mouse. Small dried pieces of valerian may be added to pot-pourri.
How to keep for later use: when the foliage yellows and begins to die in the autumn, cut it off close to the ground. Lift the roots and rhyzomes with a fork. Shake off surplus soil, split, wash and dry slowly without artificial heat.

VERVAIN

'Some write, that the water wherein this Vervaine hath beene steeped, being cast or sprinkled about the hall or place whereas any feast or banket is kept, maketh all the companie both lustie and merrie.'
Rembert Dodoens, *A New Herbal,* 1619
(trans. Henry Lyte)

Botanical name: *Verbena officinalis*   **Family:** *Asteraceae (Compositae)*
Type: HP   **Height:** 45cm (18in)
Position preferred: sunny position, any soil.
When and how to sow: sow seeds 2mm (¼in) deep in March–May.
When and how to propagate: usually by seed.
Flower colour and time of flowering: small, pale mauve flowers on upright stems in late July–August. Vervain is very insignificant as a plant until late June when it will grow as much as 45cm (18in) in a week.
Main usefulness: vervain is an anti-depressant herb of use in cases of convalescence, melancholia and depression.
Other virtues: by reputation, vervain encourages the production of breast milk.
How to keep for later use: cut the herb while in flower and dry.

VIOLET

'Love the violet, it loves you.'
Anon.

Botanical name: *Viola odorata*   **Family:** *Violaceae*
Type: HP   **Height:** 10cm (4in)
Position preferred: violets enjoy woodland conditions: dappled shade in summer, full light and sun in winter and sheltered positions. Do not plant however at the foot of south-facing walls. Violets like a woodland type soil: dig in plenty of leaf mould and compost, bone meal and sand. Violets are deep rooted so your soil should be open and well worked. Water in dry weather.
When and how to sow: violet seed needs a cold period (below 40°F) to germinate, so seed is sown in the autumn and left to winter outside. Sow in seed boxes pressing the seed into the compost. Cover the seed box with a pane of glass and leave outside all winter. In March/April introduce the tray to warmth and the seeds will soon germinate. Transplant seedlings to small pots. Plant out in autumn 21cm (9in) apart.

Violets produce two types of seed: seed pods succeed the spring flowers if these have been pollinated. The spring seeds may or may not come true to type, this depends on whether there is any cross pollination with other varieties nearby. In the summer, hanging underneath the new runners, you will find little round 'footballs' which turn reddish-brown and crack open as they ripen. The seeds inside will breed true since they are produced cleistogamously, ie self-fertilised.
When and how to propagate: take cuttings of sturdy runners which the plant produces during the late spring and summer. These will root within a few weeks and can be transplanted in the autumn to produce flowering

plants next year. If growing violets for flowers, remove all runners as they form to encourage the main plant to produce flowering crowns.

Leaf and flower colour and time of flowering: leaves are bright green, heart-shaped, small in the spring increasing in size in the summer. Flowers are deep blue, produced March–April with some flowers late autumn. Flowers are sweetly scented.

Main usefulness: violets make lovely pot plants in spring. A posy of cut flowers will scent a room deliciously. Use fresh flowers in spring salads.

Other virtues: medicinally, the dried leaves and flowers are used to treat bronchitis and catarrh. The reputation of the anti-tumour action of violets has been reported over a long period. Modern qualified herbalists use violets to treat cancers of the breast and alimentary canal.

How to keep for later use: violet leaves and flowers can be dried. The flowers lose their scent on drying. Sugar, oil and vinegar will retain the scent – so make violet syrup, violet vinegar and oil of violets. Violets can also be crystallised.

Varieties:

CZAR has scented flowers of deep purple on stems to 6cm (2½in). Leaves are light green and round. Czar is strongly growing and will flower in the autumn.

JOHN RADDENBURY flowers are blue-pale purple with white throat and short spur. Stems are 6cm (2½in) with small green leaves slightly pointed.

MRS R BARTON has white flowers with a touch of purple on the petals, and stems of 5cm (2in). The short spur is tinged purple.

PARMA VIOLETS (*V. pallida plena*) are not fully hardy and need winter protection in a cold frame. Parma violets are extraordinarily sweetly scented and have a long flowering period.

PRINCESS ALEXANDRA has scented pinky-red flowers with a yellow and white eye on a stem 6cm (21½in) long; round pointed light green leaves 5cm (2in) across.

PRINCESS OF WALES has large round flowers 2.5cm (1in) across, deep violet colour, with a white throat and no spur. Flowers are strongly scented on stems to 16.5cm (6½in).

QUEEN CHARLOTTE has scented purple flowers (not deep nor pale) with a spur of the same colour. Flowers are very erect, held above the leaves on stems of 10cm (4in). A prolific producer of seeds.

ROYAL ROBE has large purple flowers with a white throat held on a stem of 13cm (5in). Flowers are 4cm (1½in) across and strongly scented. Leaves are large, pointed and crinkled to 7cm (3in) across.

V. HIRTA produces a mass of purple flowers, alas unscented, on stems to 10cm (4in) in March/April followed by large leaves. Ideal plant to naturalise in hedges and open woodland since makes large clumps and needs no attention.

V. LABRADORICA flowers are blue with a veined white throat and unscented. The attraction is the contrast with the leaves which are reddish-green. V. labradorica is a repeat flowerer.

V. ODORATA ALBA is the white form of sweet violet. Flowers are white often tinged purple or with purple patches, scented and held on short stems. Prolific producer of seed.

V. RIVIANA is the dog violet, free flowering in spring and later in the summer. Flowers are pale-pink mauve with a deeper pink-mauve edge to a white throat. Stems to 4cm (1½in). Small bright green leaves in flowering period.

V. SELKIRKII is the great spurred violet. The flowers are lilac, veined purple on the throat, an ochre eye; the spur a deep lilac. Flowers are erect on stems 7.5cm (3in). Flowers are unscented.

WILD PANSY see Heartsease
WOODRUFF

'Like the good deeds of the worthiest persons, Sweet Woodruff delights by its fragrance most after death.'

Dr WT Fernie, *Meals Medicinal*, 1905.

Botanical name: *Galium odoratum* formerly *Asperula odorata*
Family: *Rubiaceae*
Type: HP   **Height:** 15cm (6in)
Position preferred: light, rich, well mulched soil under trees or in open borders and rockeries.

When and how to sow: sow .5cm (⅛in) deep in open ground in April; or one month earlier under glass in a seed tray.

When and how to propagate: established plants can be lifted in March and their roots divided. Replant about 30cm (1ft) apart.

Leaf and flower colour and time of flowering: narrow green leaves in successive whorls on slender erect spreading stems. Flowers are white and produced in May.

Main usefulness: leaves and flowers when dried have scent of new-mown hay. This comes from the coumarin in the plant. Dried leaves can be used in pot-pourri, and in sachets among clothes to deter insects. Sprigs of fresh leaves are added to German sparkling wine to make 'Maydrink', a refreshing drink served with sliced oranges.

Other virtues: woodruff is considered to be a diuretic and good for the stomach.

How to keep for later use: gather the leaves and flowers in May and dry.

WORMWOOD

Botanical name: *Artemisia absinthium*   **Family:** *Asteraceae (Compositae)*
HP   **Height:** 1–1.5m (3–5ft)

Position preferred: wormwood will grow in any soil and does well in dry, sandy soil. The plant spreads through its roots and can be invasive. Will grow in some shade. Wormwood dies back completely in the winter and re-appears the following spring.

When and how to sow: preferably in the autumn as soon as the seeds are ripe. Sow in drills .5cm (⅛in) in the ground; or in a seed tray. Seeds can also be sown in April and at 60°F will germinate in two to three weeks.

When and how to propagate: lift and divide established plants in March. Plant 120cm (4ft) apart if you have room, and no less than 60cm (2ft) apart.

Leaf and flower colour and time of flowering: furry, silvery grey-green leaves on erect stiff stems. Yellow flowers are produced July–August.

Main usefulness: wormwood is widely used in vermouths, liqueurs and bitters for its bitter, tonic and stomachic characteristics. Herbalists use wormwood for the same reasons to treat cases of anorexia and dyspepsia. As its name suggests, wormwood is also given in cases of worm infestation, particularly in children. Wormwood should not be used regularly since its use can become addictive.

Other virtues: use dried leaves in moth mixtures with southernwood, lavender and woodruff. Cut the stems for dried flower arrangements.

How to keep for later use: cut the flowering tops and leaves in late summer and dry.

YARROW

Botanical name: *Achillea millefolium*   **Family:** *Asteraceae (Compositae)*
Type: HP   **Height:** 60cm (2ft)

Position preferred: any soil where the drainage is adequate.

When and how to sow: in seed boxes, just pressing the seed into the surface of the compost. Sow March–May.

When and how to propagate: lift established clumps in the spring and replant rooted pieces. Once planted, yarrow grows by sending out spreading shoots. If these are kept cool and moist, they can be lifted and re-potted during the growing period.

Leaf and flower colour and time of flowering: feathery green narrow leaves, with large flat flower heads of pale lilac and white flowers in July–September.

Main usefulness: an infusion of yarrow with elderflower and peppermint is taken in case of fever or cold. Yarrow encourages the body to perspire.

Other virtues: yarrow is used by herbalists to treat cases of hypertension.

How to keep for later use: gather the herb during flowering and dry.

Appendix

Specialist Suppliers of Herb Seeds

In Great Britain:

Culpeper shops carry an extensive range of herb and wild flower seeds. These are also available by mail order from Culpeper Ltd., Hadstock Road, Linton, Cambridge CB1 6NJ. Please send a stamped addressed envelope for their free catalogues.

John Chambers, 15 Westleigh Road, Barton Seagrave, Kettering, Northants NN15 5AJ. Catalogue is free.

Suffolk Herbs, Sawyers Farm, Little Cornard, Sudbury, Suffolk, CO10 0NY. Catalogue is free.

In Canada:

Richters, Goodwood, Ontario, Canada LOC LAO. Send Can $4.00 for catalogue.

In the USA:

Abundant Life Seed Foundation, PO Box 772, Port Townsend, WA 98368. Send US $1.00 for catalogue.

Catnip Acres Farm, Christian Street, Oxford, Connecticut 06483. Send US $2.00 for catalogue.

Companion Plants, 7247 North Coolville Ridge Road, Asthens, Ohio 45701. Send US $2.00 for catalogue.

JL Hudson, Seedsman, PO Box 1058, Redwood City, California, 94064. Send US $1.00 for catalogue.

Shepherd's Garden Seeds, 7389 West Zayante, Felton, California 95018. Send US $2.00 for catalogue.